EPIQUE

The Conductor's Blueprint for Organzational Leadership and Culture in an Age of Disruption

A Jeevaganth

TABLE OF CONTENTS

THE LEADER'S BLUEPRINT IS OBSOLETE

A silent, irreversible transition has occurred. The leader's blueprint, the symbol of hierarchical authority and strategic foresight that defined management for a century, no longer builds resilient organizations. This is not a controversial opinion. It is a battlefield report from the front lines of organizations, with the signs of failure appearing as structural cracks in companies and governments across the world.

In 2023, a tremor shook the foundations of Western innovation. Microsoft, a company at the apex of global power, released data showing that a staggering 64% of its employees felt they lacked the influence to drive change. Think about that. Inside one of the world's most advanced organizations, the majority of the workforce felt their tools were useless, their creative potential wasted.

This was not a problem confined to the corporate world. The same structural cracks were appearing in the very institutions designed to manage global stability. In the chambers of the United Nations and the World Health Organization, leaders grappled with a crisis of relevance, their expert guidance struggling to compel action in a world fractured by nationalism and misinformation. Governments, meanwhile, found their multi-decade economic plans rendered obsolete overnight by supply chain shocks and energy crises, forcing them to make impossible trade-offs between climate goals, economic stability, and public health. The old blueprints for governance were failing their stress tests.

Half a world away, the same structural flaws were shattering a different, but equally powerful, "Old Playbook". For decades, leadership in Asia was a model of hyper-growth, top-down discipline, and the relentless "996" work culture. Leaders from Singapore to Seoul built their companies with absolute authority, masters of a world with cheap capital, predictable supply chains, and a seemingly endless supply of loyal talent.

Then, between 2021 and 2024, the structure didn't just groan. The foundations themselves began to collapse.

Forrest Li at Sea Group, once the architect of Southeast Asia's most valuable company, was forced to announce the death of growth at all costs, with his leadership team taking no salary until the company was saved. In South Korea, the ironclad playbook of seniority was met with the Silent Resignation of a new generation. In China, the sudden regulatory wall that halted Ant Group's IPO proved that even the most powerful builders were no longer in control of their projects.

These were not isolated incidents or failures of effort. From Seattle to Shanghai, the story was the same: world-class leaders were following the old blueprint exactly, only to find their teams no longer responding. The blueprint had not been misread. It had become a relic, describing a world that was no longer in existence.

The feeling of chaos this creates is not a failure of leadership; it is a failure of perception. For years, we described our environment as VUCA—Volatile, Uncertain, Complex, and Ambiguous. This was a useful map for a world that was changing quickly but was still fundamentally navigable. That world is gone. We are now attempting to navigate a **BANI** reality—a world that is **B**rittle,

Anxious, Non-linear, and Incomprehensible—using the outdated maps of a VUCA past. The BANI framework was developed by the American futurist, author, and Distinguished Fellow at the Institute for the Future, Jamais Cascio, to describe the chaotic and unstable environment that has become our new normal.

In a BANI world, as Cascio describes, systems don't just bend; they shatter (**Brittle**). Cause and effect are no longer reliably connected, creating deep **Anxiety** and a sense that events are **Non-linear**. And the sheer volume of interconnected variables makes the environment truly **Incomprehensible** through traditional analysis. When the old lens of management meets a world that has moved beyond mere volatility into systemic fragility, the friction we feel is the sound of a mental model breaking. To survive this shift, organizations cannot simply move faster; they must operate differently.

The Five-Front Storm: A Forensic Diagnosis

The reason these grandmasters found their tools unrecognizable is because they were standing in the center of a Five-Front Storm; a convergence of structural shifts that has permanently broken the 20th-century model of leadership. This is not a list of passing trends; instead, it is a description of the new, volatile physics of the BANI world.

Front 1 - The End of the 5-Year Plan.

The first and most foundational front of the storm is Strategic Fragility. For generations, leadership was synonymous with foresight. The five-year plan was the sacred text, a testament to a leader's ability to predict the future and chart a steady course. The core assumption was that the world, while competitive, was fundamentally stable. A well-researched plan was a fortress.

That era is over. The fortress is now a house of cards.

We have entered an age of permanent volatility, where the very act of long-term, rigid planning has become a strategic liability. The planning horizon has collapsed from years to weeks, and the "black swan" event - the unpredictable, high-impact disruption - has become the new normal. A five-year plan created in 2019 would have been rendered obsolete by a global pandemic in 2020, shattered by geopolitical conflict and supply chain collapse in 2022, and fundamentally questioned by the explosion of generative AI in 2023.

This creates a dangerous paradox: forward planning, if not constantly challenged and adapted, becomes a weakness. A rigid plan creates cognitive blindness; it trains leaders to focus on executing a predetermined path, making them incapable of seeing the profound, game-changing shifts happening right in front of them. It encourages investment in optimizing for a future that will never arrive.

The five-year plan is now a liability. The only rational response to this new reality is to abandon the pursuit of prediction and instead embrace the principles of antifragility, a term masterfully coined by Nassim Nicholas Taleb. An antifragile system is not merely resilient or robust. It is a system that actually gains strength from disorder. It feeds on volatility. We have entered an era where forward planning, if not constantly adapted, becomes a weakness.

Front 2 - The Loyalty Crisis.

The old deal, loyalty in exchange for stability, is dead. Today, that agreement has suffered a Social Contract Fracture. This is not a regional issue; it is a global schism.

In the West, the phenomenon of "Quiet Quitting" has become a dominant narrative. This is not about employees suddenly becoming lazy; it is a conscious, rational withdrawal of discretionary effort. It is the silent refusal to go above and beyond, for a system that employees feel, no longer invests in their long-term growth or well-being. They will perform the duties listed in their job description, and no more. This quiet rebellion is the Western answer to a broken contract, a deliberate rejection of the hustle culture that promised promotions but delivered burnout.

This same fracture is seen with even greater intensity in Asia. In South Korea, the "MZ Generation" is rewriting the rules of corporate life, prioritizing individual fairness and work-life balance over the old guard's demand for absolute loyalty. In China, the "Lying Flat" movement has stalled the traditional engine of ambition, as young people opt out of the gruelling 996 work culture.

The result is that the workforce is no longer a monolith; it is instead a value mosaic. Talent is now a stakeholder group demanding meaning, agency, and a return on their emotional investment. This renders traditional command-and-control power, which relies on the old contract of compliance for security, not just ineffective, but toxic.

Front 3 - What's my Value Now?

The third front of the storm is not about technology; it is about value. For the past fifty years, the career path for knowledge workers was clear - you succeeded by becoming a superior human information processor. Your value was defined by your ability to analyse data, manage complex projects, and make logical decisions faster and more accurately than others. The entire structure of middle and senior management was built on this foundation.

Now, generative and agentic AI is triggering a profound Cognitive Displacement. This is not merely the automation of tasks; it is the wholesale commoditisation of the very cognitive skills that once defined a successful manager. The domains where leaders used to demonstrate their worth, synthesizing information, identifying patterns and drafting reports, are now being handled with superhuman speed by machine intelligence. The leader whose value proposition was built on being the smartest analyst in the room has already been displaced; their core function has been outsourced to an algorithm.

This displacement signals a fundamental shift in the nature of work itself, from the static job description to the dynamic problem to be solved. The human premium is therefore the premium on orchestration. The most valuable leader is no longer the master of a single skill, but the conductor who can frame a problem worth solving and then assemble and integrate a bespoke portfolio of resources, AI agents, human specialists, and customer communities, to solve it. This is a skill that cannot be automated. It is the new pinnacle of human work, demanding that we move beyond simply managing people to orchestrating a symphony of human and machine intelligence.

Front 4 - The Trust Deficit.

The fourth front of the storm is the silent crisis created by the global shift to hybrid and remote work. This is not a logistical challenge of laptops and servers; it is the Erosion of Social Capital. For decades, the dense offices of New York, London, Singapore and Tokyo functioned as powerful engines of social capital, building trust and mentorship as a natural byproduct of daily interaction. This was the world of the chance collaboration sparked by a conversation over coffee, and the silent apprenticeship that occurred when junior employees observed a senior colleague navigate a difficult situation; both powerful byproducts of physical proximity. This ambient, relational environment was the engine of cultural learning and innovation.

The shift to remote work turned off this engine. It fundamentally altered our mode of interaction from ambient and relational to transactional and scheduled. Communication became almost entirely purposeful, confined to a 30-minute slot to achieve a specific outcome, and the trust-building in-between moments that foster psychological safety evaporated. This has created a structural debt of trust. We have been living off the social capital built up over years of in-person work, but we have lost the primary mechanism for replenishing it.

The consequences are now clear. Innovation slows as teams retreat into their digital silos. A generation of new talent, starved of the osmosis of real-world collaboration, is at risk of atrophying the very skills of negotiation, innovation, risk taking and influence that define true leadership. We are now conducting a workforce that is technically connected but socially and creatively adrift, and the bill for this structural debt has come due.

Front 5 - The New Rules of Power.

The fifth front of the storm rewrites the rules of corporate power. The era of Shareholder Primacy, where maximizing profit was the only goal, is definitively over. We have entered the age of the Stakeholder Veto, where a wide array of non-shareholder groups now holds the power to derail a company's strategy. This is not a soft trend about corporate social responsibility; it is a hard-edged shift in power dynamics.

Regulators can erase billions in value overnight, as the last-minute cancellation of Ant Group's IPO in China proved. Employees, through internal activism, can force changes to company policy. Customers can punish a brand for its perceived ethical lapses through social media fuelled boycotts. The "Move Fast and Break Things" baton, the celebrated mantra of the growth era, is dead.

This new reality means that issues once relegated to the side-desk, ESG compliance, supply chain ethics, and geopolitical positioning, have moved to the center of the boardroom. They are no longer soft options; they are the new hard constraints of commerce. A brilliant strategy that fails to account for these factors is a reckless gamble. Leaders are now, whether they like it or not, geopolitical actors, judged not just on their profit, but on their total impact on a complex and fractured world.

The Virtuoso's Dilemma

Faced with this storm, the modern organization does what it has been taught to do: it invests in mastery. Its leaders are sent to refine their technique, diligently learning the tools of the trade; the seminal works on Lean, the agile manifesto, frameworks for authentic leadership, and the latest thinking on disruptive innovation.

Each of these frameworks have provided a valuable, and often masterfully crafted, tool. They have taught teams how to optimize a process, how to structure a project, or how to lead with vulnerability. The collective effort has been a striving for individual and team-level virtuosity, driven by the belief that technical proficiency is the key to great outcomes.

When we look at the organization as a whole, however, the expected harmony is often absent. The system feels misaligned, working at cross-purposes with itself. This is **The Virtuoso's Dilemma**: the sobering realization that a collection of brilliant, highly skilled teams does not automatically create a coherent and effective organization. A mastery of individual trades is insufficient when the underlying architecture creates friction and misalignment between them.

This reveals the fundamental gap in modern organizational development: it has created master craftsmen, but it has not produced a master architect.

The agile framework, a brilliant tool for the software team, creates stress fractures when it clashes with the rigid structure of the finance and compliance departments. A leadership technique that encourages empathetic coaching is undermined by a corporate performance system that still only rewards individual outputs. The organization has been trying to solve a systemic, architectural problem with the isolated skills of specialist trades.

This flawed approach leads to a common, systemic mistake - the treatment of change as a separate, episodic event. Change management becomes a distinct discipline, a difficult renovation project to be managed after a new strategy is designed. An attempt is then made to force the organization to adopt the new model. This is fundamentally backward. In an era of permanent volatility, an organization's capacity for change cannot be a special project; it must be its core design principle.

The specialised tools that have been mastered are not wrong; they are simply being applied to the wrong problem. They are tools for optimizing the parts of a predictable construction, not for designing a resilient, adaptive structure capable of weathering a storm. The solution, therefore, is not another specialised tool to manage a temporary change. The solution is a new master blueprint for the organization itself.

The Promise of a New Blueprint

The solution to the Virtuoso's Dilemma isn't to manage with more force, but instead to find a new way to build. It lies in a new master blueprint; a unified, timeless framework for designing a resilient, adaptive culture capable of performing amidst the chaos of the Five-Front Storm. This is not another specialised tool to add to the toolbox. It is a new way to see, design, and lead the entire organization.

This framework is built on five core habits that, which when cultivated in balance, form the structural foundation of any high-performing, adaptive, resilient organization.

This is the **EPIQUE** framework.

Empathy. The ability to understand the unstated needs of your customers and your people. This, combined with Innovation, is the antidote to Cognitive Displacement.

Pragmatism. The discipline to confront reality as it is, not as you wish it to be. This is the antidote to Strategic Fragility.

Innovation. The courage to explore the unknown and the discipline to learn from failure. This is the Engine of Adaptation.

Quality. The relentless pursuit of excellence and the creation of systems that build trust. This is the antidote to the Erosion of Social Capital.

Engagement. The commitment to creating a sense of shared ownership and purpose. This is the antidote to the Social Contract Fracture.

These are not a checklist of corporate values. They are the five fundamental pillars of organizational integrity. The problem in most organizations is that some pillars are overbuilt, while others are crumbling, creating a dangerous imbalance.

Therefore, the first step is to develop the ability to see this imbalance, with precision. This requires a new diagnostic lens, one that moves beyond isolated employee surveys or financial metrics. We call this tool the **EPIQUE Resonance Profile**. Its purpose is to render a single, holistic picture of an organization's cultural dynamics—revealing its inherent strengths, its hidden weaknesses, and the critical relationships between them. It is the leader's equivalent of an architect's structural analysis, designed to show which pillars are load-bearing, which are underdeveloped, and where the stress fractures are beginning to form.

Our journey together is straightforward and practical.

In **Part 1**, we will explore the five EPIQUE habits in depth, grounding each one in foundational research and revealing what they look like in action.

In **Part 2**, we shift from theory to practice. Here, we unpack the diagnostic used to generate your EPIQUE Resonance Profile. With this new clarity, we then apply the powerful logic of the Theory of Constraints to identify the single Constraining Habit, the weakest pillar, holding your entire structure back. Finally, we move to a rigorous playbook for making the First Push, the precise, high-leverage intervention that begins to reinforce the foundation.

The storm you are facing is real, and the old maps are obsolete. The feeling of chaos is not a failure of leadership; it is a failure of perception, and understanding, that cripples your ability to navigate a BANI world. What is required is not a better way to manage the old structure, but a new blueprint to constantly build and rebuild a more resilient one.

It is time to become the architect.

PART 1

THE FIVE PILLARS OF THE BLUEPRINT

CHAPTER 1

THE HABIT OF PRAGMATISM: THE COURAGE TO SEE REALITY

You are the captain of a ship.

It is a good ship, powerful and fast, with a proud history and a talented crew. You have a clear destination marked on your map, a destination handed down from the board and promised to your shareholders - Transformation, Growth, Market Leadership. The sky is clear, the sea is calm, and the latest reports from the engine room are positive. From the bridge, everything looks perfect.

But you have a gnawing feeling you can't shake. It is not something you can prove with a chart or a number. It's a subtle change in the air, a strange, unfamiliar current you feel under the hull. Your sophisticated instruments, the quarterly P&L statements, the market share data, the glossy employee engagement surveys, all flash green. They all tell you to push ahead. But your intuition, the seasoned, hard-won instinct that got you this far, is screaming that a storm is coming. A big one.

This is the Captain's Dilemma. And it is the core, unspoken anxiety of modern leadership.

We are living in an age of profound contradiction. We are

drowning in data but starved for reality. We have dashboards that can track a thousand metrics in real-time, yet we have never been more disconnected from the unvarnished truth of our customers' lives and our employees' lived experiences. We are told to be agile, to be innovative, to be resilient. We are given a thousand maps, a thousand management theories, a thousand "seven-step solutions" from charismatic gurus. But none of them address the fundamental, terrifying problem: our ship's navigation system was built for a world that no longer exists. It is designed to operate in the relatively calm, predictable seas of the years gone by, but we are living in an age of hurricanes.

The old system rewards you for having the best map, a detailed, five-year strategic plan that is predicated on a world that has moved on. The new reality demands that you have the best compass, a reliable, internal guidance system that allows you to navigate as and when the map is continually rendered useless by the storm.

Let's explore the design for that compass.

It is not another way finder to a mythical treasure island of success. It is a guide to rebuilding your ship's core navigation system from the inside out. It is about upgrading your organization's fundamental operating rhythm—shifting from merely surviving the storm to harnessing its energy. While competitors cling to the soggy, outdated maps of a vanished world, you will use the turbulence to reach your destination with greater speed and precision.

Rather than offering another set of rigid processes, we explore a new set of mental models. A more sophisticated way to orient your organization to reality. This framework is called EPIQUE. It is a compass built on five interdependent habits, five cardinal directions for leadership in the 21st century.

The first of these habits, the magnetic north of the compass and the foundation upon which all others depend, is the **habit of Pragmatism**.

Pragmatism is the foundational bearing of the EPIQUE framework. Before any journey can be charted, the ship's compass must be calibrated to a single, objective, and non-negotiable direction: True North. That direction is reality. Without it, what follows is not navigation, but a confident and accelerating journey in the wrong direction.

The Paradigm Shift: The Twin Blades of Pragmatism

Pragmatism is a word that has been worn smooth by misuse. In the modern corporate lexicon, it has often become a synonym for being practical, cheap, fast, or even unprincipled; a convenient justification for taking shortcuts or compromising on quality to meet quarterly targets. This is not the Pragmatism we speak of. This is a reductionist interpretation of a powerful concept.

True Pragmatism, in the context of leadership, is a radical, courageous, and disciplined commitment to seeing things as they actually are, not as you wish it were - allowing you to then act decisively with true reality. It is a discipline of both perception and action, of seeing and doing. Like a spearhead forged from two interlocking blades, one is useless without the other. A leader who sees reality clearly but fails to act is a strategist of the void. A leader who acts decisively without a clear view of reality is simply a gambler, and the house always wins in the end.

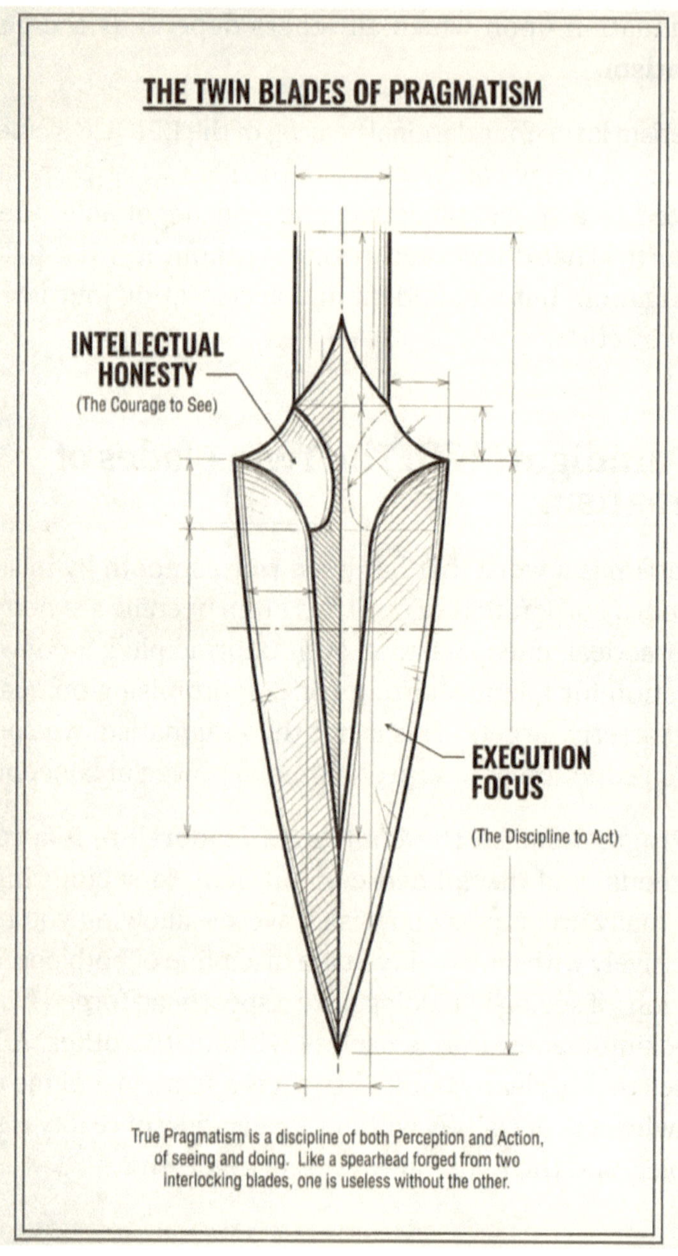

The Twin Blades of Pragmatism are
intrinsically intertwined, and reinforcing.

Intellectual Honesty

The first blade is Intellectual Honesty. This is the raw courage to see reality. It is the discipline to confront what Jim Collins, in his seminal work Good to Great, called the brutal facts of your current reality. In his exhaustive study of companies that made the leap from mediocrity to sustained excellence, Collins discovered a fascinating paradox in their leaders. On one hand, they maintained an unwavering, almost religious faith that they would prevail in the end. On the other, they were brutally, almost obsessively, honest about the grim realities of their present situation.

He named this the Stockdale Paradox, after Admiral Jim Stockdale, who survived seven and a half years as a prisoner of war in Vietnam. Stockdale observed that the first to die were the optimists, those who clung to the false hope of being out by Christmas. They died of a broken heart. Stockdale survived by accepting the brutal fact of his reality while never losing faith in the final outcome.

In an organizational context, intellectual honesty is the cultural equivalent of Stockdale's mindset. It is the institutional humility to accept that your opinion, no matter how senior your title, is not a fact. It is the active courage to seek out disconfirming evidence. This was the genius of Andy Grove, the legendary CEO of Intel. Grove built a culture of constructive confrontation, a disciplined system for harnessing conflict to find the truth. At Intel, the rule was simple - anyone could challenge an idea, regardless of rank, as long as they were armed with data and logic. Meetings were not a stage for the highest-paid person's opinion to win; they were a crucible where ideas were stress-tested against reality. This relentless, depersonalized pursuit of truth was more important than the preservation of hierarchy. It was this cadence of constructive confrontation that allowed Intel to navigate seismic shifts in the technology landscape that destroyed its less honest competitors.

Execution Focus

The second blade, inseparable from the first, is Execution Focus. This is the discipline to act on reality. Seeing the world clearly is worthless if you do nothing about it. The corporate graveyard is filled with companies like Kodak and Xerox, who saw the future with perfect clarity but failed to act on that vision.

An execution focus is the spirit captured in Deng Xiaoping's famous aphorism: "It doesn't matter if a cat is black or white, so long as it catches mice". This is more than just a folksy saying; it is a profound declaration of what truly matters. Deng used this idea to pull China out of the dogma of rigid ideology and onto a path of pragmatic progress. For a leader, it is a mandate to prioritize outcomes over sacred cows, results over elegant theories, and effectiveness over internal politics. It is the discipline to ask, "Does this really work?" and to ruthlessly discard what doesn't, regardless of who sponsored it or how much has been invested in it.

This philosophy is perfectly complemented by the wisdom of Peter Drucker, the father of modern management. He stated, "There is nothing so useless as doing efficiently that which should not be done at all". This is the ultimate critique of a purely process-driven organization. An organization can be a model of efficiency, perfectly executing it's (flawed) strategy, and still fail spectacularly.

Drucker's insight reveals the true synergy of the twin blades. Intellectual Honesty is the discipline that identifies the right mice to catch, while Execution Focus is the skill that ensures the cat actually catches them.

Therefore, the two blades must be seen as a single, inseparable system for effective leadership. The relationship is not additive; it is multiplicative. A leader who possesses perfect Intellectual Honesty but lacks an Execution Focus is not a failed philosopher; he is a failed leader. Such clarity is useless, a strategic vision that withers on the vine. Conversely, a leader who is a master of Execution but lacks Intellectual Honesty becomes a dangerous engine of waste, efficiently mobilising resources to solve the wrong problems and marching the organization with great discipline towards a cliff. The ultimate measure of a leader is not just the quality of their vision or the power of their execution, but the product of the two.

The Proof: A Story of Water and Will

In 1965, a small, tropical island was thrust into an unwanted independence. It was a tiny nation with no natural resources, a fractured multi-ethnic population, and hostile neighbours. It had no army to defend itself and no economic reason to exist. But its most terrifying vulnerability was not military or economic. It was water.

The island of Singapore had almost no fresh water of its own. It was almost entirely dependent on a single pipeline from its larger, and at times unfriendly, neighbour, Malaysia. The water agreement was set to expire in the coming decades, and Malaysian politicians frequently used the threat of "turning off the tap" as a political weapon. For Singapore, water was not a commodity; it was an existential threat.

A leadership team in denial of the facts or one that was indifferent would have responded in predictable ways. They might have denied the severity of the threat, hoping for the best. They might have engaged in endless, fruitless negotiations, kicking the can down the road. They might have focused on short-term, politically popular solutions like subsidizing water costs, making the problem worse.

But Singapore's founding leader, Lee Kuan Yew, was a pragmatist of the highest order. His most well know mantra was "find out what works and to do it". He and his team embodied the twin blades of Pragmatism.

First, they practiced radical Intellectual Honesty. They confronted the brutal facts of their existence. They saw that their nation's survival depended on two critical vulnerabilities: a lack of natural resources, most critically water, and a lack of a credible defence to protect their sovereignty. They understood that any solution to the water problem would be meaningless if their larger, more powerful neighbours could simply impose their will. They saw that their national survival was threatened by a two-headed dragon: a physical dependence on the supply of water, and a military vulnerability that made them susceptible to coercion.

They did not sugarcoat this reality. Instead, they made it a national obsession. They launched public campaigns to frame water not as a utility, but as a precious, life-giving resource. Every citizen was made aware of the nation's vulnerability. Simultaneously, they instituted national military service and began the long, arduous process of building one of the most technologically advanced and well-trained armed forces in the region. This was the ultimate act of pragmatism - ensuring that any threat to "turn off the tap" would carry an unacceptable high price. The military deterrent provided the security and the time for the water strategy to mature.

Second, with the shield of a credible defence being built, they demonstrated a ferocious Execution Focus on the water problem itself. They did not bet on a single solution. Instead, they created a diversified, multi-pronged national strategy known as the Four National Taps. This was not just a policy; it was a declaration of war on their own vulnerability.

The first tap was to maximize the water they could import, securing existing agreements. This was the practical, short-term reality.

The second tap was to relentlessly expand its own water catchments. They transformed the entire island into a sponge, paving roads with porous materials, building canals, and turning two-thirds of the nation's land into a water catchment area. This was a massive, decades-long engineering feat.

The third tap was the most audacious. They invested heavily in desalination, a technology that was, at the time, prohibitively expensive. They knew the cost of the technology would fall over time, and they were willing to pay the stupid tax of being an early adopter to master the process. They were executing for a future reality, not just the present one.

The fourth and final tap was the masterstroke of pragmatic innovation - NEWater. This was a project to recycle sewage water into ultra-clean, potable drinking water. The technological challenge was immense, but the psychological barrier was even greater. The "yuck factor" was a significant political risk. A less pragmatic leader would have avoided it. But Singapore's leaders understood the reality - they needed every drop. They invested in a public education campaign, building a state-of-the-art visitor center to explain the science, and branding the recycled water with a clean, futuristic name. Lee Kuan Yew himself drank a bottle of NEWater on national television to demonstrate his confidence.

Today, Singapore is a global leader in water technology. The threat that once defined its vulnerability has been transformed into a source of national strength and a valuable export industry. The story of Singapore's water is the story of Pragmatism in action. It is a story of confronting a brutal fact with intellectual honesty and then pursuing a solution with a relentless, multi-generational focus on execution.

The Five Levels of Pragmatic Maturity

The journey from denial to adaptation is not just a change in process; it is a fundamental evolution of an organization's character. An organization's relationship with reality, its level of Pragmatism, can be seen as a five-stage maturity model. Each level reveals a distinct personality, a different way of seeing and interacting with the world. By understanding these five levels, you can hold up a mirror to your own organization and ask: "Who are we, really?"

The Ostrich. At the lowest level, we find The Ostrich. This is the Denying Organization. Its defining character is fear. Like an ostrich burying its head in the sand, it believes that what it cannot see cannot hurt it. This organization actively rejects uncomfortable truths. Bad news is suppressed, either explicitly or through subtle cultural cues. Messengers of bad news are labelled as "not team players" or "negative influencers". The leadership lives in an echo chamber, surrounded by optimistic projections that bear little resemblance to reality. Failure is hidden or blamed on external factors. The Ostrich's mantra, spoken or unspoken, is "Don't bring me problems, bring me solutions," a phrase that sounds empowering but in practice effectively shuts down the flow of critical, unfiltered information from the front lines. This culture mistakes silence for stability, not realizing it is the silence of a system that has stopped learning.

The Debater. One step up the ladder is The Debater. This is the Aware Organization. Its character is one of intellectual vanity. At this level, the organization is no longer in denial. People are generally aware of the major problems. In fact, they are often experts at discussing them. The issues are the subject of endless hallway conversations, sophisticated PowerPoint presentations, and cynical jokes in team chat channels. The elephant in the room is not invisible; it is the subject of a well-attended weekly seminar. A collective learned helplessness pervades the culture, masked by the appearance of intellectual activity. The problems are seen as too big, too political, or simply the way things are here. The act of studying a problem becomes a substitute for the act of solving it, creating the illusion of progress without any of the risk.

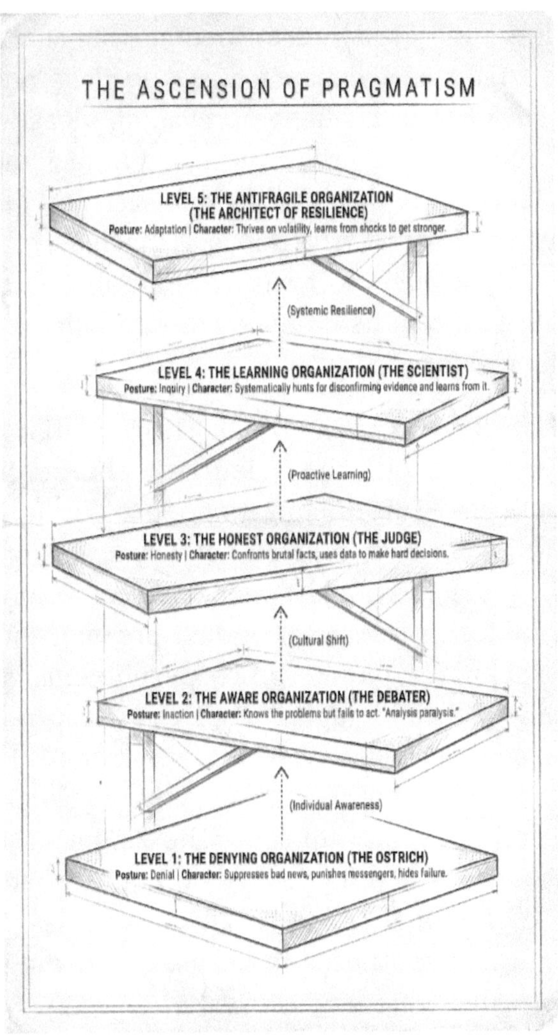

The journey to Pragmatism is a five-level evolution of organizational character, from the fearful Ostrich to the visionary Architect of Resilience.

The Arbiter. The crucial turning point in the journey is reaching Level 3, where the organization becomes The Arbiter. This is the Honest Organization. Its character is defined by integrity. The Arbiter values truth above all else. It confronts the brutal facts. In meetings, data and evidence are valued far more than opinion and hierarchy. The highest-paid person's opinion is just that, an opinion, unless it is backed by data. Meetings are characterized by rigorous, depersonalized debate focused on ideas, not on people. Individuals feel safe to challenge prevailing ideas without fear of personal reprisal. The Arbiter is skilled at facilitating honest debate, protecting the process from politics and personalities, synthesizing disparate information, and making a clear, decisive call based on the evidence. It ensures that all voices are heard, but it understands that its ultimate responsibility is to render a verdict and move forward.

The Scientist. Beyond honesty lies The Scientist. This is the Learning Organization. The Scientist's character is one of relentless curiosity. This organization moves beyond just being honest about its current reality; it actively seeks to improve its understanding of it. It is not just open to disconfirming evidence; it hunts for it. Teams regularly conduct pre-mortems on major projects, a technique pioneered by psychologist Gary Klein, where they ask, "Let's imagine it's a year from now and this project has failed spectacularly. What went wrong?". This exercise bypasses the social cost of seeming negative and liberates people to identify potential risks upfront. The Scientist treats every action as an experiment and every outcome, good or bad, as a rich source of data. It frames challenges not as problems to be solved, but as hypotheses to be tested, turning the entire operation into an engine for discovery.

The Architect. Finally, at the pinnacle of Pragmatism, is The Architect of Resilience. This is the Antifragile Organization. Its character is one of visionary foresight. Drawing on the powerful concept of antifragility from the scholar and risk analyst Nassim

Nicholas Taleb, this organization is not just resilient to shocks, meaning it can withstand them. It is antifragile: it actually gets stronger from them. Every crisis, every market shift, every unexpected failure is treated as a valuable, free lesson that provides energy for growth and evolution. The Architect of Resilience is no longer just managing the response to a single crisis. It is focused on building a system, a culture, a set of processes, a mindset, that is inherently adaptive. This is the essential posture for a BANI world, as it designs an organization that does not fear volatility, but in fact thrives on it, knowing that every brittle fracture in the market is an opportunity to out-learn the competition and redefine the game.

Calibrating the Compass: How to Measure Pragmatism

Understanding the five characters of Pragmatic maturity provides a powerful new vocabulary. It allows you to hold up a mirror and ask, "Who are we, really?". But to move from a simple gut feeling to a robust diagnosis, a more structured approach is needed. This is not about finding a single, numerical score, but about learning to think like a master diagnostician. It is about using a credible triangulation of evidence from independent, yet interconnected lenses, to provide you a clarity of the situation.

The first lens is **Perception**, the subjective story of what your people "Say" about the culture of Pragmatism. The second is **Behaviour**, the objective evidence of what your organization actually "Does", as seen in project data, meeting outcomes, conversations and personnel decisions. The third and most crucial lens is **Structure**, the underlying "Shape" of the organization, the systems, incentives, and processes that dictate the path of least resistance and explain why the behaviour occurs.

The true story of your culture is found not in any single lens, but in the friction between them. When you synthesize these three viewpoints, you can see the invisible forces at play. You may find a culture where people say they value truth (Perception), but where zombie projects are never killed (Behaviour). The third lens reveals why. For example, the company's bonus system punishes any admission of failure (Structure). This chasm between the stated aspiration and the systemic reality is the "Gravity Gap". This is the powerful, invisible force that pulls behaviour back to the old ways, no matter how inspiring the rhetoric. Seeing your organization in these three dimensions is the very essence of seeing reality. It moves you beyond treating the symptoms (the behaviour) and allows you to diagnose the disease (the structure). This holistic perspective is the only credible starting point for meaningful change.

Your First Act of Pragmatism

This framework is not just an academic model. It is a mirror and a map. It gives you a language to diagnose your own culture and a direction for improvement. But reading about it is not enough. The journey to Pragmatism begins, as it must, with a single, pragmatic act.

That act is not to reorganize your team or to launch a new initiative. It is a quieter, more personal decision. It is the decision to stop assuming and start diagnosing. It is the choice, in your next meeting, to be the one who asks the uncomfortable question. It is the choice to value an uncomfortable truth over a comfortable half-truth. The rest of this book will give you the tools to climb the ladder, but the first step must be taken now, in your own mind. It is the commitment to see.

The Pocket Summary

- The greatest leadership failure is choosing a comfortable lie over an uncomfortable truth. The antidote is Pragmatism.

- True Pragmatism is a weapon with two blades: Intellectual Honesty (seeing reality) and Execution Focus (acting on reality).

- Organizations mature through five levels of Pragmatic Character, from the fearful Ostrich to the visionary Architect of Resilience.

- As a leader, you do not need to have all the answers, but you must have the courage to confront the brutal facts, starting with yourself.

Three Questions for Your Team

1. What is one "brutal fact" about our business, our market, our organization, our team's performance that we are all politely avoiding in our meetings?

2. Think of a recent project that failed or underperformed. Did we conduct an honest, blame-free post-mortem to learn from it, or did we quietly bury it and move on?

3. Looking at the five characters, who are we really? The Ostrich, The Debater, The Arbiter, The Scientist, or The Architect? What is one specific thing we could do next week to start acting like the next level up?

Conclusion: The Courage to See

The journey to Pragmatism begins, as it must, with a single, pragmatic act: the organizational decision to stop accepting the world as it is presented and to start seeing it as it truly is. This chapter has provided the blueprint for that journey. The **Twin Blades** of Intellectual Honesty and Execution Focus are the core principles of action for an effective organization. The **Five Characters** serve as a mirror for diagnosing the organization's current stance toward reality. And the **Three Lenses** of Perception, Behaviour, and Structure provide the diagnostic method for seeing the "Gravity Gap" between the organization's aspirations and its underlying systems.

These are not just academic models. They are the foundational components of a truly adaptive organization. They are the tools for calibrating the entire ship's compass to True North. The rest of this book will explore the other tenets on the EPIQUE compass, but they are all built upon this bedrock. Without an organizational culture grounded in the courage to see reality, the empathy we will explore next is merely sentiment, and the innovation that follows is just a gamble. The first, most crucial step for any organization is always the collective commitment to see.

CHAPTER 2

THE HABIT OF EMPATHY: THE DISCIPLINE OF PERSPECTIVE

In the last chapter, we established that Pragmatism is the foundational bearing of an effective organization: a radical, courageous commitment to seeing the world as it is, not as we wish it were. A pragmatic organization builds its strategy on the bedrock of reality.

But what is reality?

An organization that defines reality only by what can be measured on a dashboard - sales data, market share, operational metrics - is looking at a black-and-white photograph of a vibrant, multi-dimensional world. It sees the what but is blind to the why. It sees that a product's usage has dropped but doesn't understand the user's silent frustration that caused it. It sees that employee turnover is high but cannot feel the undercurrent of burnout that is driving its best people away.

This is the trap of surface-level pragmatism. It mistakes data for truth. An organization that operates on this incomplete picture is constantly surprised by the market, blindsided by cultural issues, and perpetually reacting to events it should have seen coming. It is a ship navigating with a chart that shows the coastlines but omits the powerful, invisible currents of human motivation that will ultimately determine its fate.

To achieve profound Pragmatism, an organization must go deeper. It must build the systemic discipline to seek not just the data of what is happening, but the human and systemic context of why it is happening. This requires the second, inseparable habit of the EPIQUE framework: Empathy.

The Shift: From User Insight to Ecosystem Mastery

For decades, the most forward-thinking organizations have been on a quest to better understand their customers. This journey has given rise to two powerful disciplines. The first is that of Design Thinking. This is a methodology that provides a structured process for innovation by immersing teams in the user's world. The second is the "Jobs to Be Done" (JTBD) theory. This provides a powerful lens for that inquiry, shifting the focus from product features to the customer's underlying struggle for progress.

These tools are, without question, revolutionary for understanding the user. Their limitation, however, is not in their design, but in their scope. They are built to solve a contained problem for an individual, leaving them less equipped to address the messy, complex emotional and systemic residue that permeates our world; the widespread distrust in institutions, the anxiety of economic uncertainty, or the cultural shifts created by new technologies. This is the smog in the ecosystem that a single, clean product solution cannot fix.

This is where we must introduce a new, higher-order capability - Systemic Empathy.

The Blueprint of Systemic Empathy

Systemic Empathy is not a replacement for Design Thinking or JTBD; it is the essential foundation that makes them effective at a macro-organizational level. It is the discipline of mapping and navigating the entire ecosystem, and it operates on three distinct pillars.

The first pillar requires a shift in perspective from the User to the Ecosystem Participant. While a sophisticated JTBD analysis considers the social context of a user's job, its primary focus remains centered on the end-user to drive product innovation. It is not designed to be a tool for macro-organizational diagnosis. Systemic Empathy, picks up where JTBD leaves off, and expands the aperture. It takes the same powerful "what is the job?" lens and deliberately applies it to the entire ecosystem—inwards towards employees and outwards towards suppliers, partners, and regulators. It operates on the understanding that an organization's success is determined by the interplay of all these actors. It moves beyond the user, to ask the critical systemic question: "How does one person's 'job' create friction or opportunity for others?" This reveals macro-opportunities for platform-level solutions rather than isolated point-products.

Secondly, we need to move from looking only at the consumers to understanding the non-consumers. JTBD is excellent at explaining why people hire a current solution. Systemic Empathy, however, is also interested in the far larger market of non-consumers, those who aren't hiring any solutions yet. Systemic empathy investigates if the cost of participating in the current ecosystem is emotional, social, or financial. It seeks to understand the residue of distrust or anxiety that prevents them from even entering the market. This is where true market creation lives.

Finally, an organization must move from Present Needs to Future Sentiments. While JTBD focuses on stable needs over time, Systemic Empathy leverages on what psychologist Daniel Goleman has termed **Cognitive Empathy**. This is the ability to rationally understand and predict another's perspective and feelings. This allows an organization to anticipate how major social and technological trends will change how people feel about their jobs. It asks: "In an AI-driven world, how will my need to feel valued and wanted by my company change?" or "How does hybrid work change the 'job' of being a manager?" By applying Cognitive Empathy at a macro level, an organization can skate to where the puck is going, designing for future sentiments before the industry shifts.

Systemic Empathy, therefore, is the organizational capability to feel the entire system in all its complexity. It is the discipline that prevents an organization from building a perfect solution for a single user that is ultimately rejected by the messy, interconnected and fast-evolving reality of the world.

To see this capability in action, we now turn to a story of farmers and frequencies. The following case study of the Vietnamese telecommunications company, Viettel, is a masterclass in the architectural power of Systemic Empathy. It will serve as a concrete illustration of the three conceptual pillars we have just established: the strategic shift from a single user to the entire ecosystem, the market-creating focus on non-consumers, and the visionary leap from serving present needs to building for future sentiments.

The Proof: A Story of Farmers and Frequencies

In the early 2000s, Vietnam's economic miracle was largely confined to its bustling cities. The vast rural countryside was a sea of non-consumers for the global telecommunications industry. Sophisticated market models, viewing the rural population as isolated users, saw only poverty and dismissed the market entirely. They saw the data but were blind to the ecosystem.

But one company, the state-owned Viettel, approached the

problem differently. Instead of starting with a user-centric product idea, they began with a systemic inquiry, sending their teams to live in the villages to understand the deep emotional and systemic residue at play. They applied the immersive principles of Design Thinking not just to a user, but to an entire ecosystem.

First, they moved from user to ecosystem participant. They saw that the job of a mother in a village was not an isolated need. Her desire to feel secure about her son in the city was intrinsically linked to the job of a farmer who needed to get a fair price for his crops by accessing market information, and the job of a fisherman who needed to ensure the safety of his community by warning of a coming storm. They realized they were not solving a problem for a single user; they were building a platform to reduce the systemic friction for an entire community. This ecosystem-level view, born from a systemic application of empathetic inquiry, revealed a macro-opportunity that a purely user-focused analysis would have missed.

Second, this deep immersion allowed them to address the massive market of non-consumers. The global giants saw a population that was too poor to afford a phone. Viettel, through empathy, saw a population whose irregular, seasonal cash flow made the standard monthly subscription model an impossible financial burden. The non-consumption was not due to a lack of desire, but to a high financial and accessibility cost. This insight led them to pioneer the sale of cheap, pre-paid SIM cards in tiny denominations, sold at every village stall. They didn't try to sell a product to a broken market; they created a new market by designing a business model that was empathetic to the financial reality of the non-consumer.

Finally, they moved from present needs to future sentiments. They understood that simply providing a connection was not enough. As the country developed, the job of a mobile network would evolve. Leveraging cognitive empathy, they predicted that as their customers' economic lives improved, their need for data, for internet access, for a bridge to the digital economy, would become as important as the initial need for a voice call. This foresight led them to take the huge strategic risk of building a nationwide, data-ready network from the outset. They were not just solving the present need for a phone call; they were building a platform for the future aspirations of an entire nation.

Viettel's competitors had better technology and more money. But Viettel possessed a more powerful strategic weapon. They used Systemic Empathy to see the entire ecosystem, to unlock the vast potential of the non-consumer, and to build for the sentiments of the future. They didn't just win a market; they created one.

The Viettel story provides a powerful, real-world demonstration of Systemic Empathy's strategic value. By expanding their view from the individual user to the entire community, they uncovered a platform opportunity their competitors missed. By focusing on the reasons for non-consumption, they designed a business model that created a new market. And by anticipating future sentiments, they built a network that secured their long-term dominance. This illustrates a crucial distinction between Systemic Empathy and another powerful field of inquiry.

The Distinction: Systemic Empathy vs. Behavioural Insights

At this point, a leader versed in modern management science might ask a critical question: How does this concept of empathy differ from the powerful and popular field of Behavioural Insights? It is a question that deserves a clear and precise answer, for the distinction reveals the unique role that Systemic Empathy plays in organizational strategy.

The field of Behavioural Insights, built on the Nobel Prize-winning work of psychologists like Daniel Kahneman and economists like Richard Thaler, is a revolutionary discipline. It has given us a profound understanding of the cognitive biases and the predictable irrationalities, that shape human decision making. It is a powerful tool for redesigning systems to help people make better choices.

The two disciplines are complementary, but they operate with a different primary lens. To understand the difference, imagine a person who is consistently failing to cross a narrow bridge over a deep canyon.

A practitioner of Behavioural Insights would focus on the psychology of the crossing. They might diagnose that the person is exhibiting loss aversion, an irrational fear of the fall, and then nudge them toward a better choice. They might redesign the system by painting the bridge to look wider, adding higher handrails, or offering a small reward for reaching the other side. Their goal is to make it easier for the person to overcome their bias and successfully cross the bridge.

A practitioner of Systemic Empathy, however, would start by asking why the person needs to cross the canyon at all. They would focus on the necessity of the crossing. Through inquiry, they might discover the person's job is to get food that is only available on the other side. They might then realize the true systemic friction is not the scary bridge, but the fact that there is no food on this side of the canyon. Their solution would not be to redesign the bridge, but to reposition the food.

This reveals the fundamental difference in their starting points. The diagnostic lens for Behavioural Insights is the cognitive bias. The diagnostic lens for Systemic Empathy is the unmet human need. While Behavioural Insights is a powerful tool for optimizing how people make choices, Systemic Empathy is a tool for understanding why they feel the need to make those choices in the first place. It provides the deeper, foundational diagnosis that allows a leader to move beyond influencing behaviour and begin the work of solving the fundamental human problems that drive it.

The Empathy Maturity Model: From Ignorance to Insight

An organization's ability to practice Systemic Empathy is not a simple "on or off" switch; it is a deep-seated capability that evolves over time. This evolution can be understood as a five-stage journey of organizational character, a deliberate progression from a state of wilful blindness to one of profound, boundary-less connection. Each level reveals a more sophisticated ability to see the world through the eyes of the ecosystem. By understanding these five distinct characters, you can hold up a mirror to your own organization and ask the fundamental question: Who are we, really?

The Fortress (Posture: Ignorance). At this level, the organization is a fortress, its gaze turned perpetually inward. It operates on the belief that its internal logic is superior to the messy reality of the outside world. Customer feedback is dismissed as anecdotal, and employee concerns are seen as noise. The organization is blind, and worse, it is proud of its blindness, mistaking its ignorance for strategic focus.

The Analyst (Posture: Data Collection). The Analyst organization has recognized that the outside world matters, but only as a source of data. It obsessively collects the what; survey scores, purchase histories, website clicks, but remains disconnected from the why. It creates detailed charts about customer behaviour but has never had a deep conversation with an actual customer. It is an organization that can describe the world with clinical precision but has no real understanding of it.

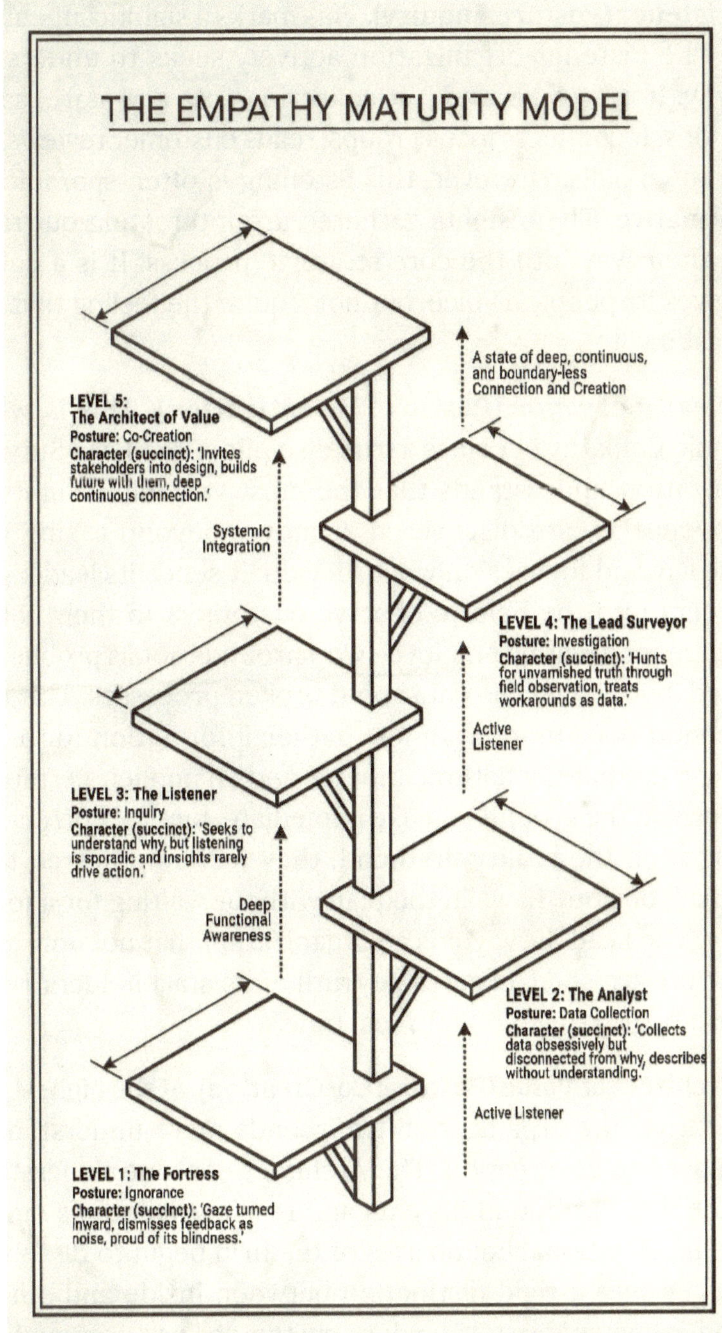

The Empathy Maturity Model – From Ignorance to Insight

The Listener (Posture: Inquiry). This marks a significant cultural shift. The Listener organization actively seeks to understand the why. It moves beyond just collecting data and starts asking questions. It conducts focus groups, reads customer reviews, and holds town halls. However, this listening is often sporadic and performative. The insights gathered are interesting but rarely make their way into the core strategic process. It is a culture that gives its people a voice, but not a quite the feeling that they can cast a vote.

The Lead Surveyor (Posture: Investigation). This is where Systemic Empathy becomes a true discipline. The Lead Surveyor organization understands that the most valuable insights are not given; they are discovered. It moves beyond asking what people say and focuses on what they do. It sends its leaders and engineers into the field to observe customers in their natural environment, treating employee workarounds not as problems to be fixed, but as valuable data about broken processes. This deep immersion does more than just gather information for a later strategy; it creates a natural impetus and an implicit permission for those on the ground to make immediate, tactical corrections. Having seen the reality firsthand, they feel empowered to fix the small, obvious flaws in the plan without waiting for a formal review. The Lead Surveyor is an organization that not only hunts for the unvarnished, observable truth of its stakeholders' reality but also begins to act on it in real time.

The Architect of Value (Posture: Co-Creation). At the highest level of maturity, the organization transcends mere understanding and moves to co-creation. The Architect of Value understands that the most profound insights and resilient solutions emerge when the traditional boundaries of the firm begin to dissolve. It no longer sees a rigid distinction between inside and outside. Instead, it invites key stakeholders, customers, partners, and even critics directly into the heart of the design process. Customers and employees are no longer subjects to be studied, but are treated as essential partners in creating value. Feedback loops are not just a data-gathering exercise; they are the core circulatory system of the product development and strategic planning processes. The organization is no longer just solving problems for its stakeholders; it is building the future with them. This is the pinnacle of Systemic Empathy: a state of deep, continuous, and boundary-less connection and creation.

The Empathy Audit: A Practical Framework

Understanding the five characters of maturity provides a powerful new vocabulary for diagnosis. But to move from a subjective feeling to a robust, evidence-based conclusion, a more structured approach is needed. This is not about finding a single, numerical score. It is about learning to think like a master diagnostician by applying the Three-Lens Diagnostic across the full, systemic scope of the organization.

The first lens is Perception. This captures the subjective story of what stakeholders say. A true audit of Systemic Empathy gathers these perceptions from the entire ecosystem. It looks outward to understand whether customers and partners feel that their needs are met. It investigates the narratives that non-consumers tell themselves about the product or service that prevent them from participating. And it turns inward to gauge whether employees feel equipped and empowered to serve customers, or if they express frustration and cynicism.

The second lens is Behaviour. This examines the objective evidence of what the organization actually does. This lens demands a rigorous, ecosystem-wide review of data. Outwardly, it analyzes product usage patterns and support ticket resolution times to see if they align with the brand promise. For non-consumers, it investigates their current behaviours to identify the inefficient workarounds they employ in the absence of a good solution. As critically, it scrutinizes internal behaviour. Does the leadership spend time understanding their stakeholders and customers, or is it consumed by internal meetings? Are truth tellers about product flaws promoted or managed out? This is where an organization's true priorities are revealed.

The third and most crucial lens is Structure. This audits the underlying systems and incentives that shape all perception and behaviour just observed. This is the ultimate "why". Outwardly, an organization's product architecture can create friction for customers, just as its legal framework can create adversarial relationships with partners. For non-consumers, the industry's pricing model or distribution channels may be the source of their structural exclusion. And inwardly, the budgeting process can systematically starve the very projects that would serve customers best, while the performance management system may reward employees for closing a support ticket quickly, even if the customer's problem remains unsolved. This chasm between the stated aspiration and the systemic reality is the gravity gap, the powerful, invisible force that pulls behaviour back to the old ways. Seeing an organization through these three lenses, applied across the entire system, allows the organization to move up the maturity ladder.

Your First Act of Empathy

A framework is a map, not the journey. The path to Systemic Empathy begins not with a major initiative, but with a single, conscious act: the decision to move from abstract analysis to direct observation and immersion.

This first act is not to reorganize or to launch. It is the quieter choice to create a space for unmediated reality to enter the organization. It is the decision to spend less time debating what stakeholders *might* want, and more time in their world, observing what they actually do. This could be a leadership team reviewing the raw, unfiltered comments on an employee survey, or an engineering team watching a video of a new user struggling, in silence, with the software they just built.

The goal is not to solve or to defend. The goal is simply to see. It is the organizational equivalent of placing an empty chair in a meeting, a silent reminder of the reality that exists outside the firm's walls. This is the first, essential step in calibrating the organization's compass to the human world it claims to serve.

The Pocket Summary

- True Pragmatism requires more than data; it requires a deep understanding of the human context. The discipline for acquiring this understanding is Systemic Empathy.

- Systemic Empathy is not a soft skill. It is a macro-organizational capability for seeing the entire ecosystem—inwardly at employees, outwardly at customers and partners, and at the non-consumers who are structurally excluded.

- Organizations mature through five levels of empathetic character, from the blind Fortress to the boundary-less Architect of Value.

- The first act of Systemic Empathy is not to solve, but to create a space for unmediated reality to enter the organization through direct, judgment-free observation.

Three Questions for Your Team

1. When was the last time we, as a team, directly observed a customer or an employee struggling with a process we designed, without interrupting to explain how it is supposed to work?

2. What is one common complaint from our customers or partners that we internally dismiss as an outlier or user error, and what might that complaint be telling us about a flaw in our own system?

3. Looking at the five characters, who are we really? The Fortress, The Analyst, The Listener, The Lead Surveyor, or The Architect of Value? What is one specific thing we could do next week to start acting like the next level up?

Conclusion: The Bridge from Insight to Action

The habit of Pragmatism gives an organization the courage to see reality. The discipline of Systemic Empathy gives it the wisdom to understand that reality in all its messy, human complexity. It is the capability that moves an organization from the what of data to the why of data.

By expanding the empathetic lens from the user to the entire ecosystem—from present needs to future sentiments, and from external stakeholders to the organization's own internal reality—a leadership team can see the whole board. They can identify the hidden frictions and the unstated needs that are the true source of both risk and opportunity.

But this deep, systemic understanding, as powerful as it is, is inert on its own. An architect's blueprint does not build a cathedral. A conductor's score does not perform a symphony. The insight gained through Systemic Empathy is merely potential energy. To give it force, to translate that understanding into collective action and commitment, requires the next crucial habit.

It is time to energize the system. Therein lies the value of the next crucial habit, the habit of Engagement.

CHAPTER 3

THE HABIT OF ENGAGEMENT: THE ARCHITECTURE OF SHARED COMMITMENT

An organization grounded in Pragmatism and informed by the deep insights of Systemic Empathy possesses the most valuable asset in modern business: a clear and accurate lens through which to see the world. With this lens, the organization can perceive the true nature of the market, the unstated needs of its customers, and the hidden frictions within its own systems. From the architect's office, the path to creating value looks clearer than ever before.

But a lens, no matter how powerful, does not build a skyscraper. People do. A lens provides clarity, but it does not, by itself, create action. The process of translating this newfound clarity into a physical reality is not a simple, one-way transmission of instructions. It is a dynamic, two-way act of Engagement.

This is where we must refine our understanding of how these habits interact. The lens of Systemic Empathy provides the raw, unfiltered view of the ecosystem—the customer's struggle, the employee's friction, the partner's frustration. But this clarity is inert if it remains the property of a few senior leaders. It is merely potential energy.

Strategic Engagement, therefore, is the engine that converts the potential energy of this clarity into the kinetic force of collective action. An organization that attempts to act on insight without this engine will inevitably fail. Its clarity, no matter how brilliant, will remain the property of a few, and its solutions will be met with quiet compliance rather than passionate commitment. The active intelligence of the workforce—the very engine of adaptation and growth—will remain dormant.

This reveals the true architectural role of the habit. Strategic Engagement is the disciplined process of taking the clarity revealed by the lens and bringing it into the organization to be debated, pressure-tested, and forged into a shared, collective commitment. It is the work of building the collaborative structure that allows the entire crew to understand the mission, improve upon the plan, and execute it with a shared sense of purpose and pride. It is the discipline that transforms a clear insight into a living, evolving reality.

The Shift: From Compliance to Commitment

For decades, the dominant logic of management was built on a simple, mechanical view of human motivation: a philosophy of if-then rewards. If you hit your sales target, then you get a bonus. If you complete the project on time, then you get a reward. This carrot and stick approach treats human beings like simple machines, assuming that applying an external stimulus will produce a desired output.

This model works reasonably well for simple, algorithmic tasks with a clear set of rules. But the moment a task requires even a rudimentary level of cognitive skill, creativity, or judgment, the if-then model faulters and in some cases, it does more harm than good.

This is not a matter of opinion, but a counter-intuitive truth grounded in a half-century of social science. The research, powerfully synthesized by author Daniel H. Pink in his seminal work, Drive, reveals a consistent and startling pattern. Foundational experiments by Edward Deci in the 1970s, later confirmed by landmark studies at institutions like the London School of Economics, all converge on the same conclusion: for the creative, problem-solving work that defines the modern economy, traditional if-then rewards do more than just fail to motivate—they can actively decrease performance, stifle creativity, and extinguish intrinsic drive.

The old playbook is not just outdated; it is actively sabotaging your team's potential. To build true, sustainable engagement, we must architect a system built not on external rewards, but on a deeper, more powerful set of intrinsic drivers.

To achieve true engagement, leaders must upgrade their mental model to Motivation 3.0. They must shift their focus from securing temporary compliance to fostering enduring commitment. This requires tapping into the three powerful, intrinsic drivers that are already present in every human being.

Autonomy. The first is Autonomy. This is our innate human desire to be self-directed, to have control over our own lives and work. A leader who fosters autonomy doesn't micromanage every detail. They are tight on the "what" and the "why", but loose on the "how". They set clear goals and define the boundaries, but they give their people freedom in how they achieve those goals. They trust their team to find the best path. This is the difference between telling someone "Lay these bricks exactly as I've shown you" and "We need to build a strong, beautiful wall that will stand for a century; do you think this is the best way to do it?"

Mastery. The second is Mastery, our innate urge to get better at things that matter. People have a deep-seated desire to learn, to grow, and to feel a sense of progress in their craft. A leader who fosters Mastery provides opportunities for their people to develop their skills. They assign "Goldilocks tasks"—challenges that are not so easy that they cause boredom, nor so difficult that they cause anxiety, but are just right to stretch a that person's unique set of abilities, and to pull them into a state of deep focus. They provide constructive feedback and celebrate progress, not just victory, creating an environment where people can become true craftsmen, not just hired hands.

Purpose. The third, and most powerful, key is Purpose. This is our universal yearning to be part of something larger than ourselves. People are most deeply engaged when they understand how their individual effort contributes to a meaningful, overarching goal. This is the lesson of the cathedral builder. A leader who fosters purpose is a master storyteller, a Chief Meaning Officer who constantly connects the daily work of the team to the organization's North Star, its mission, its vision, and the positive impact it has on the world.

A leader who masters the art of Engagement understands that their primary job is not to motivate people. The desire for Autonomy, Mastery, and Purpose is already there. Their job is to create the conditions where people can motivate themselves.

The Proof: A Story of Shoes and Soul

In the late 1990s, the online shoe market was a joke. The conventional wisdom was that no one would ever buy shoes without trying them on first. The logistics were a nightmare, the return rates would be crippling, and the established brick-and-mortar retailers had an insurmountable advantage.

Into this environment stepped a young entrepreneur named Nick Swinmurn. He had a simple, frustrating experience: he couldn't find a specific pair of brown Airwalks at his local mall. He had an idea: what if there was a single online store that sold every style, every colour, every size of shoe?

He pitched the idea to venture capitalists. They laughed him out of the room. The idea was impossible.

But Swinmurn was a pragmatist. He decided to run an experiment. He went to his local shoe store, took pictures of some shoes, and posted them on a simple website. If someone ordered a pair, he would run back to the store, buy the shoes at full retail price, and ship them himself. He was losing money on every sale, but he was gaining something far more valuable: proof. Proof that people would buy shoes online.

With this proof, he secured a small amount of seed funding from a man named Tony Hsieh. Hsieh, who had recently sold his own company to Microsoft, was intrigued. Together, they founded a company called Zappos.

From the very beginning, Hsieh understood that Zappos was not really a shoe company. It was a customer service company that happened to sell shoes. This was their North Star. Their purpose was not to move units; it was to deliver "WOW" through service.

This purpose became the foundation for a culture of extreme engagement. Hsieh and his team made a series of radical decisions that were completely at odds with conventional business practice.

First, they fostered radical Autonomy. They famously empowered their call center employees—or "Customer Loyalty Team"—to do whatever it took to make a customer happy. There were no scripts. There were no time limits on calls (the company record is over 10 hours). If a customer needed a specific shoe that Zappos didn't have, the employee was encouraged to search a competitor's website and direct the customer there. They were given the ultimate trust and freedom to serve the customer.

Second, they invested heavily in Mastery. New employees went through an intensive, four-week training program that was less about the mechanics of the job and more about immersing them in the company's history, philosophy, and ten core values. At the end of the training, the company made a now-famous offer, known as "The Offer." They would offer each trainee several thousand dollars to quit on the spot. The goal was to weed out anyone who was just there for a paycheck. It was a powerful filter for commitment.

Third, and most importantly, Hsieh was a relentless architect of Purpose. The mission to "deliver WOW" was not just a slogan on a poster; it was the central organizing principle of the entire company. Every decision, from their famously free shipping and 365-day return policy to the design of their warehouse, was made with the goal of serving that purpose. They published a "Culture Book" every year, an unedited collection of employees' thoughts on the company culture, to keep the purpose alive and authentic.

The result was a level of employee engagement that was legendary. Zappos became famous for its fanatical customer service and its passionate, almost cult-like employee base. The company grew at a dizzying pace, and in 2009, it was acquired by Amazon for $1.2 billion.

The Zappos story is a powerful testament to the commercial power of engagement, with an overlay of systemic empathy. They succeeded in an "impossible" market not because they had a better logistics system or a fancier website, but because they built a culture where every single employee was deeply, personally, and emotionally engaged in the shared purpose of delivering happiness to their customers.

The Framework: The Five Characters of Engagement Maturity

Engagement is not a binary state; it is a spectrum. Organizations evolve from a culture of pure command-and-control, where people are treated like machines, to one of deep, shared ownership, where people act like partners. Each level has a distinct character.

The journey to Engagement is a five-level evolution of organizational character, from the transactional Mercenary to the passionate Steward.

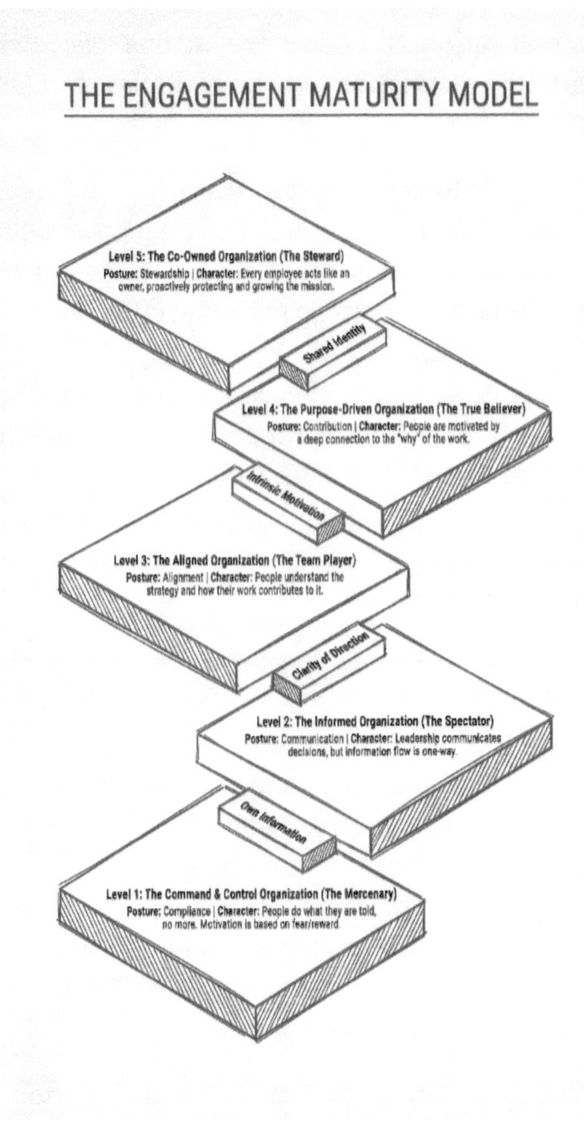

Five Characters of the Engagement Maturity model

The Mercenary Command and Control Organization. At the bottom is The Mercenary. This is the Command & Control Organization. The Mercenary's character is transactional. They are there for the paycheck. They do what they are told, no more, no less. Their loyalty is to their own self-interest, not to the organization's mission. Information is hoarded at the top.

The primary motivational tools are fear and financial reward. There is a clear and rigid distinction between "thinkers" (management) and "doers" (employees).

The Spectators – Informed Organization. Next is The Spectator. This is the Informed Organization. The Spectator's character is passive. This organization is not as secretive as the Command & Control Organization. Leadership makes an effort to communicate its decisions and strategies. However, the information flow is almost entirely one-way. Employees are told what is happening, but they are rarely asked for their input. They may be on the pitch playing the game, but their minds are merely watching from the stands; disempowered to influence the game. They might cheer if the team is winning, but they feel no personal responsibility for the outcome.

The Team Player – Aligned Organization. A significant shift occurs when the organization creates The Team Player. This is the Aligned Organization. The Team Player's character is cooperative. This is the first level of true engagement. Leadership goes beyond just communicating the strategy; they work hard to ensure that every individual understands how their specific work contributes to the bigger picture. They use tools like OKRs (Objectives and Key Results) to create a clear line of sight from daily tasks to the company's highest-level goals. The Team Player knows their position, understands the game plan, and executes it reliably.

The True Believer – Purpose Driven Organization. A deeper level of engagement is achieved with The True Believer. This is the Purpose-Driven Organization. The True Believer's character is one of passion. This organization has successfully tapped into the powerful intrinsic motivators of Mastery and Purpose. Leaders are not just managers; they are coaches who help their people grow. More importantly, they are master storytellers who constantly reinforce the "why." The True Believers are not just aligned; they are motivated. They are not just playing a position; they are playing for the love of the game.

The Steward – Co-owned Organization. Finally, at the pinnacle, is The Steward. This is the Co-Owned Organization. The Steward's character is one of profound responsibility. In this organization, the line between management and employee begins to blur. Every individual feels a deep sense of psychological ownership over the company's mission and its success. They don't just perform their role; they act like owners. They proactively identify problems and opportunities far outside their formal job description. They protect the company's resources as if they were their own. The Steward is not just playing for the love of the game; they feel like they own the team.

The Hijacking of Engagement: From Active Process to Passive Metric

Before we can explore the drivers of true engagement, we must first reclaim the concept from a dangerous misconception that has taken root in modern management. In many organizations today, the word "engagement" has been hijacked. It has been transformed from a dynamic, active process into a passive, administrative metric.

This is most clearly seen in the rise of the annual engagement survey. This tool, often owned by the HR department, has become synonymous with the concept itself. It is treated as a way to feel the pulse of the people, which in practice has come to mean measuring their happiness and satisfaction. Are the salaries competitive? Are the perks good? Is the stress level low? The survey results are compiled into a score, and managers are then tasked with improving their engagement score. This often translates into a series of targeted initiatives designed to improve specific scores.

This is a profound strategic error. It mistakes a diagnostic for a solution and a feeling for a function.

Strategic Engagement, in its true and powerful form, is not a passive metric to be measured; it is an active, architectural process to be led. It is not about gauging happiness. It is about removing friction and channelling energy. It is the rigorous work of understanding the systemic obstacles that prevent talented people from doing their best work, and helping those who are behind the curve to perform with pride. It is about re-architecting the system to create new pathways or remove barriers. It is the discipline of connecting the work to be done with the intrinsic motivation of the people who must get the job done.

An organization focused on the modern, corrupted version of engagement asks, "Are our people happy?" An organization practicing Strategic Engagement, however, asks a much more powerful and pragmatic question: "What is standing in the way of our people doing their best work on our most important goal?"

The first question creates comfortable passengers. The second creates committed co-pilots. The goal of Strategic Engagement is not to improve a survey score by managing feelings. The goal is to build a relentless, self-correcting engine for progress by removing obstacles and creating systems that work.

The Engagement Audit: A Four-Lens Diagnostic

How, then, does a leader then add a layer to the happiness score and diagnose the true state of engagement in their organization? The answer is to stop treating engagement as a feeling to be measured and start treating it as a systemic capability for achieving results. This requires a rigorous, architectural investigation that moves from subjective feeling to objective result, and finally to the root cause. This is a four-lens diagnostic.

Lens 1: Perception (The Claim). The audit begins with the subjective reality of the team. This lens seeks to understand how people feel about their work and their connection to the organization's goals. This is the domain of tools like targeted surveys or structured "Stay Interviews". We are not asking about general happiness. We are asking focused questions: "Do you feel connected to the mission? Do you believe you have the autonomy to do your best work? Do you see a clear path for your contributions?" This data is the starting hypothesis. It is what the people in the system claim to be true.

Lens 2: Behaviour (The Reality). A feeling of empowerment is not the same as effective action. This lens, therefore, seeks to validate the claims of the first by looking at objective, undeniable evidence of how work actually gets done. Using tools like Organizational Network Analysis (ONA), we can map the real-world patterns of communication and collaboration. This provides an evidence-based picture of the organization's true circulatory system. It cuts through the noise of what people say to reveal what they actually do. The gap between Perception and Behaviour, where a team says it is collaborative but the data shows it is siloed, is often the first sign of a significant structural problem.

Lens 3: Outcome (The Result). A team can feel good and appear busy, but still fail to produce meaningful results. This third lens asks the crucial question: "So what?" It measures the tangible outcomes that is the ultimate purpose of engagement. This is not about a single KPI. It is a multi-dimensional view of performance: Are our projects succeeding or failing? Is the quality of our work improving? Are we building stronger relationships with customers and partners? Are we generating valuable new ideas? This lens connects the internal dynamics of Perception and Behaviour to the external reality of performance. It answers the question: "Are the team's feelings and actions actually helping the organization win?"

Lens 4: Structure (The Intervention). This final lens provides the segway to building solutions. After understanding the full chain, from feeling (Perception), to action (Behaviour), to result (Outcome), the leader can now move from diagnosis to intervention. This is where the leader acts as a true architect, asking the fundamental question: "What, or who, have we failed to engage?" This question forces an examination of the entire organizational structure and its connections to the wider ecosystem. A failed product launch, for instance, may reveal a failure to engage with end-users during development. If innovation is slow, perhaps the structure has failed to connect talent with senior strategists. If customer churn is high, it may be because the system has failed to properly engage customer service teams with product development teams, preventing crucial feedback from flowing.

This approach is a practical application of the organizational learning theory known as Double-Loop Learning, pioneered by Harvard's Chris Argyris. Single-loop learning asks, "Are we doing things right?" and seeks to fix deviations from the existing process. This is what most managers do. Double-loop learning, however, asks, "Are we doing the right things?" It challenges the underlying assumptions, goals, and structures of the system itself. By asking "What have we failed to engage on?", the leader is practicing double-loop learning. We are not just trying to fix the bad outcome. We are questioning the very design of the system that produced it. This transforms the leader from a manager who maintains the current system into an architect who redesigns it for superior performance.

The Call to Action: The First Diagnostic Test

Engagement cannot be commanded, nor can it be bought with perks. It can only be cultivated by architecting a system where it can flourish. The first act of the architect, therefore, is not a grand speech or a new initiative. It is a quiet, deliberate diagnostic test. It is the first application of the four-lens audit to a specific, critical organizational challenge.

Instead of launching another broad engagement program, select a single, high-stakes outcome that is currently at risk. This could be a struggling product line, a critical project that has lost momentum, or a persistent failure to innovate in a key market. This becomes the focus for the first audit.

With this focus established, the organization begins the disciplined work of moving through the four lenses. It starts by gathering data not on general happiness, but on how the team feels about (Perception) their ability to achieve this specific outcome. It then seeks out objective evidence of how the team is actually collaborating, or failing to collaborate, in pursuit of the goal (behaviour). This is followed by a sober assessment of the actual outcome, confronting the unambiguous results, or lack thereof.

This process culminates in scrutinising the supporting structures for this project; meeting schedule, team configuration, funding and so on. Armed with a clear understanding of the gap between perception, behaviour, and the disappointing outcome, the leader can now ask the crucial architectural questions: To achieve this outcome, who do we need to connect with? What is preventing them from collaborating effectively? Is it a failure to engage the right teams? A failure to engage with the customer? A failure to engage with a critical piece of market data?

This is the leader's first true architectural test. It is not a conversation; it is an investigation. The insights gathered are not casual feedback; they are the raw data that reveals where the existing organizational design is succeeding and where it is failing. This is the first, crucial survey of the terrain upon which a culture of true, sustainable engagement will be built. It is the moment the leader stops managing feelings and starts architecting for results.

Pocket Summary

- **Redefine Engagement:** The common definition of engagement as "employee happiness" is a strategic error. True Strategic Engagement is not a passive feeling to be measured, but an active, architectural process for achieving a specific outcome.

- **Stop Managing Feelings, Start Architecting Systems:** The leader's role is not to make people happy, but to design a system where talented people can achieve meaningful goals. The focus must shift from reaction to architecture.

- **Use the Four-Lens Diagnostic:** A rigorous audit is required to move from symptom to solution. This involves analyzing Perception (how people feel), Behaviour (what they do), and Outcome (the results they get) to diagnose the root cause in the Structure (the organizational design).

- **Ask the Right Question:** The ultimate architectural question is not "Are my people happy?" but "What, or who, have we failed to engage on?" This question, applied to a specific strategic goal, reveals the design flaws that are truly holding the organization back

---

Three Questions for Your Team

1. What is the single most important outcome our team must deliver in the next quarter, and do we all describe that outcome in the same way?

2. What is the biggest obstacle—a process, a meeting, a missing piece of information—that is currently making it harder for us to achieve that specific outcome?

3. If we could change one rule about how our team is allowed to collaborate with other parts of the organization, what change would have the greatest impact on our success?

Conclusion: The Engine of Execution

The Habit of Engagement, therefore, is not a quest for employee satisfaction, but the architectural work of building an engine for execution. It is the discipline of channelling the collective energy of the organization towards its most critical goals. It transforms the abstract insights from Empathy and Pragmatism into tangible results by creating a system where talented people are relentlessly focused on a shared objective; this grows employee satisfaction at the organic level.

This architectural work begins with a rigorous diagnostic. By moving beyond the happiness score and applying the four-lens audit, a leader can get a true, evidence-based picture of the organization's health. By analyzing the chain of causation from Perception to Behaviour to Outcome, they can identify the root flaws in "the Structure", or the organizational design, that are preventing success. This process replaces guesswork with diagnosis, and allows the organization to intervene with precision.

To put this in context, Pragmatism provides the destination and Empathy provides the map of the human terrain, while Strategic Engagement is the engine that drives the vehicle forward. It is what unlocks human energy and focuses it on the journey, transforming a compliant workforce into a committed and effective one.

But what happens when this newly engaged, focused team, executing flawlessly against the plan, encounters a problem for which no plan exists? What happens when the blueprint itself is revealed to be incomplete in the face of market volatility or a disruptive competitor? To solve problems that have never been solved before and to adapt in the face of true uncertainty, an organization needs more than just a powerful engine for execution. It needs a system for discovery. This requires the fourth habit: Innovation.

CHAPTER 4

THE HABIT OF INNOVATION: THE ENGINE OF ADAPTATION

Your ship is sound. Its design grounded in the reality of Pragmatism. Your navigation is true, guided by a deep Empathy for the currents and the ports you serve. Your crew is committed, powered by a shared sense of Engagement. You are executing your current voyage with masterful skill.

But the blueprint that made your ship best-in-class is already becoming obsolete.

On the horizon, new vessels are appearing faster, more efficient, designed according to a completely different set of architectural principles. The very definition of a port is changing, as new islands of opportunity rise from the sea while old, familiar harbours lose their relevance. In this world, being a master captain of today's ship is not enough. You must also become the Naval Architect of tomorrow's fleet, capable of designing your next vessel while the current one is still at sea.

This is the true challenge of Innovation.

Innovation is perhaps the most worshipped and least understood concept in businesses and organizations. We are told to think outside the box, to disrupt, to fail fast. These slogans are plastered on corporate walls and repeated in boardrooms, but they have become cliches and are rarely translated into meaningful action. For some, innovation is a theatrical performance, confined only to brightly lit "innovation lab" in the corner of the office, filled with beanbag chairs and whiteboards, that produces a flurry of sticky notes that only occasionally has real-world impact. It's a hackathon that generates some fun ideas that are promptly drowned by Monday morning's to do list.

This is not Innovation. This is innovation theatre. While there will be times when this theatre produces great plays, we need a more reliable system.

Sustainable Innovation is not a single event, a creative workshop, or the heroic act of a lone genius. It is a habit. It is a deeply embedded, systemic capability for continuous adaptation. It is the engine that allows your organization to learn, evolve, and reinvent itself, not just once, but over and over again, in multiple overlapping loops, achieving a kinetic stability in sustained growth and readiness for the future. It is the discipline of turning uncertainty from a threat into an opportunity.

If the first three habits allow you to master the present, the Habit of Innovation is what allows you to earn the right to have a future.

The Shift: From "More of the Same" to "Something New"

Why do so many successful, well-managed organizations fail to innovate? Why did Blockbuster, the undisputed king of home video, see Netflix coming and do nothing? Why did Kodak, the inventor of the digital camera, get crushed by digital photography?

The answer is one of the most powerful and tragic paradoxes in business, a phenomenon the late, renowned Harvard professor Clayton Christensen famously termed The Innovator's Dilemma.

Christensen's research revealed a shocking truth: doing

everything right according to the principles of good management is precisely what leads to failure. Good managers are taught to listen to their best customers, invest in projects that promise the highest returns, and focus on their most profitable market segments. This is a recipe for success in a stable market. But it is a recipe for suicide in the face of disruptive change.

Blockbuster's best customers wanted a wider selection of new releases at their local store, not a clunky, mail-order DVD service with a limited catalogue. Kodak's most profitable customers were professional photographers who demanded higher-quality film, not grainy, low-resolution digital images. By listening to their best customers and focusing on their most profitable products, these companies optimized themselves into oblivion. They were so focused on making their existing engine bigger and more powerful that they failed to see that the world was about to switch to electric motors.

This is the trap of sustaining innovation. Sustaining innovation is about making good products better. It's about adding more features, improving quality, and cutting costs. It is a vital and necessary activity for any healthy business. But it is not enough.

To survive and thrive over the long term, organizations must also master disruptive innovation. Christensen describes this as the most misunderstood and powerful force in business. Disruptive innovation is not about making better products for your best customers. It is about creating a new foothold at the bottom of the market or in a completely new market. A new market that a good dose of Systemic Empathy will unveil to you.

Disruptive innovation rarely begins with a frontal assault. It is a subtler, more insidious strategy that starts by targeting the customers the market leaders don't want. It begins by creating a product that is simpler, more affordable, and more accessible; a product that the incumbents, with their high-end features and fat profit margins, invariably dismiss as inferior. This dismissal is their fatal mistake. The first personal computers were not better than the powerful mainframes of their day; they were scoffed at as toys for hobbyists, and in doing so, they created an entirely new market from scratch. In the same way, early Japanese steel mini mills didn't challenge the giants on high-quality structural steel. They attacked the forgotten, low-profit segment of the market: cheap rebar. The big steel companies were happy to cede this junk business, not realizing that the disruptors were using it as a beachhead from which to learn, scale, and eventually, launch an attack on the entire industry.

In both cases, the disruptor established a foothold and then relentlessly improved, moving upmarket until the once-dominant leaders were displaced. The first digital cameras were not better than film cameras; they were terrible in comparison. But they were more accessible—they allowed you to see your picture instantly, for free. That accessibility created a new market, and from that foothold, they improved until film became a niche for nostalgists and artisans.

The profound challenge for any leader is that the very systems and cultural values that make an organization good at sustaining innovation - efficiency, quality control, listening to top customer - actively kill disruptive ideas. A disruptive idea, in its infancy, always looks like a joke. It has lower profit margins, serves a smaller, less important market, and its performance is worse than the established product. Without a deliberate process that seeks out and assesses the value of these seemingly irrational opportunities, the organization's success becomes a gilded cage, leading it to rationally optimize its way into obsolescence.

And so, the organization's immune system, designed to protect the core business, attacks the new idea and destroys it.

To break this cycle, leaders must perform a difficult mental shift. They must stop seeing innovation as a single activity and start seeing it as a complete eco-system with three distinct, interconnected layers. They must become architects of an organization that can do two contradictory things at once: run its existing business with ruthless efficiency, and explore the uncertain future with the freedom of a startup.

The Framework: The Three Layers of an Innovative System

A culture of innovation is not a magical mist that descends upon an organization. It is a system that must be designed and built with intention. This system has three layers: the psychological **Drivers** that fuel the human desire to create, the procedural **Method** that provides the tools for discovery, and the structural **Management** that creates a safe space for new ideas to grow.

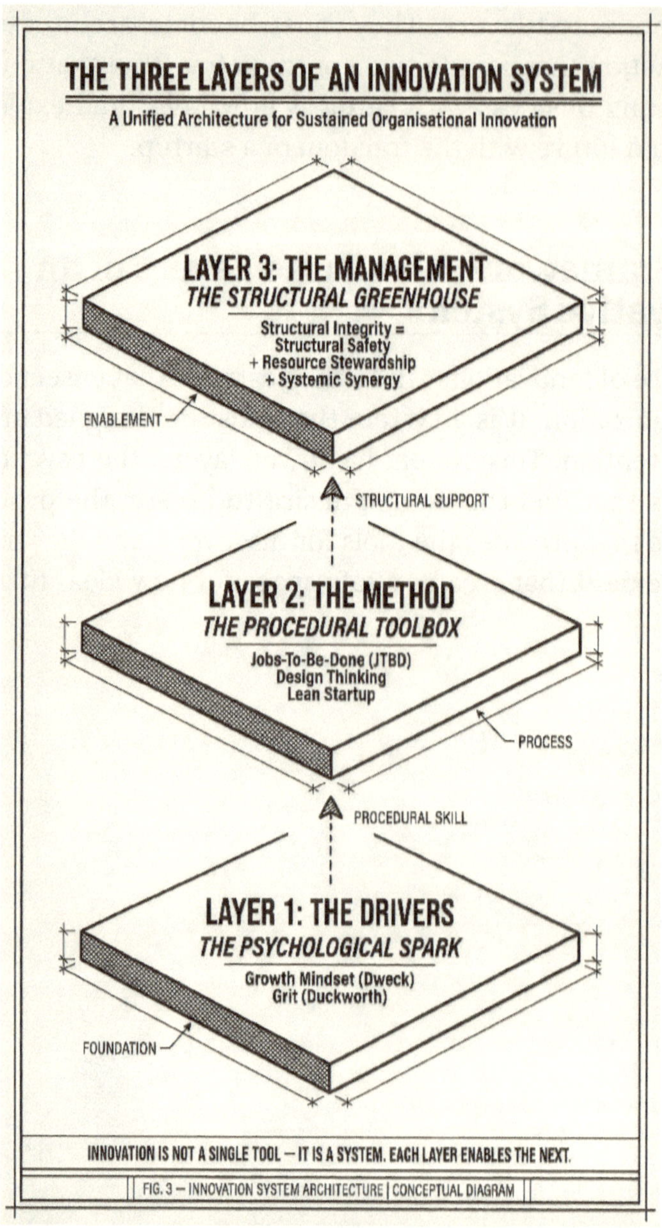

Sustainable innovation is a complete system. It requires the human "Spark" of motivated individuals, the procedural "Toolbox" of the right methods, and the structural "Greenhouse" of a supportive management system.

The Drivers

The first layer of the innovation system is The Drivers. This is the raw, foundational human energy required for any creative act to begin and endure. It is the psychological engine of discovery. This engine is not a single component, but a powerful combination of two forces: a collective mindset that embraces challenge and a shared resilience that overcomes adversity. An organization must architect itself to cultivate both.

The first force is what Stanford psychologist Carol S. Dweck calls the Growth Mindset. This is the fundamental belief that abilities and intelligence are not fixed traits but can be developed through dedication and hard work. In an organizational context, this is far more than a leadership slogan; it is a systemic belief embedded in processes. An organization with a collective Growth Mindset sees a failed experiment not as a mark of incompetence to be punished, but as a valuable asset—data purchased through intelligent effort. It designs its review processes to ask "What did we learn?" before, or if ever, asking "Who is to blame?" It promotes individuals who stretch themselves and learn from setbacks, not just those who deliver predictable, incremental wins. This creates what Microsoft CEO Satya Nadella calls a learn-it-all culture, the only fertile soil in which the seeds of true innovation can germinate.

The second force is Grit, a concept powerfully articulated by psychologist Angela Duckworth. Grit is the unique combination of passion and perseverance applied toward long-term goals. It is the stubborn resilience required to navigate the valley of despair; the inevitable period of doubt, failure, and resistance that all novel ideas must traverse. From an architectural perspective, Grit is not just an individual's responsibility. The organization's structure must be designed to sustain its own drive; its own Grit. This means creating funding mechanisms that are demand driven, and not quarterly. It means providing executive sponsorship that acts as a shield against premature criticism. It means celebrating the perseverance of a team that is still iterating on a hard problem, not just the victory of a team that has already crossed the finish line.

These two drivers are symbiotic. A Growth Mindset without Grit leads to a culture of "interesting conversations" where ideas are explored but never pursued with the tenacity required to make them real. Grit without a Growth Mindset leads to teams stubbornly pursuing a flawed plan, unable to learn from failure and adapt their approach. An organization architected for innovation does not simply hire for these traits; it builds a system where a Growth Mindset is the default and Grit is the rational and rewarded response to any meaningful challenge.

The Method

This brings us to the second layer, The Method. If The Drivers are the engine of innovation, The Method is the steering wheel and the GPS. It is the disciplined process that channels raw energy in a productive direction. The quest for a single, universal "innovation process" is therefore a fool's errand. This is like a master carpenter insisting on using only a hammer for every job. A true innovator, like a master craftsman, has a full toolbox and possesses the wisdom to know which tool to pick for each specific task.

An innovative organization doesn't have a process; it has a portfolio of processes, a set of distinct disciplines of inquiry. Let's examine three of the most powerful.

First, when the primary challenge is the need to understand a deep-seated, unarticulated human need, the right tool is Design Thinking. This is not a rigid, linear process, but a philosophy of inquiry rooted in the ethnographic methods of anthropology. As practiced by firms like IDEO, its power lies in its insistence on moving beyond what people say to what they actually do. For example, when Swiss-based medical device company Medela wanted to improve their hospital-grade breast pumps, they didn't just run focus groups with nurses. A team of designers spent days observing them in neonatal intensive care units. They noticed nurses were constantly juggling pumps, babies, and clipboards, and had developed awkward, inefficient workarounds. The designers' key insight was that the nurses' problem wasn't the pump's performance; it was the lack of a flat, stable surface to place things on. This led to the creation of a new pump with a simple, flat top that doubled as a workspace. It was a small change, born not from a survey, but from deep, empathetic observation. That is the work of Design Thinking.

Second, when the primary challenge is a problem of validation—when you have a new product idea but are uncertain about its core assumptions—the right tool is The Lean Startup. Developed by Silicon Valley entrepreneur Eric Ries and heavily influenced by the work of Steve Blank, this methodology is a direct assault on the old model of writing a detailed business plan and then spending months or years building a product in secret. The Lean Startup argues that for a new venture, the most critical activity is not building; it is learning. Its core loop is a rapid cycle of Build-Measure-Learn. You start by identifying your riskiest assumption (e.g., "Will people trust a stranger to sleep in their spare bedroom?"). Then you build a Minimum Viable Product (MVP)—the smallest, fastest, cheapest version of your idea that allows you to test that assumption. This is what the founders of Airbnb did. They didn't build a global booking platform; they took pictures of their own apartment, put them on a simple website, and tested the core assumption that people would pay to stay in a stranger's home. The data they gathered from that simple MVP was infinitely more valuable than any market research report. That is the work of The Lean Startup.

Third, when the primary challenge is a problem of strategy—when you are trapped in a hyper-competitive market where everyone is fighting over the same customers—the meaningful tool is Blue Ocean Strategy. Developed by INSEAD professors

W. Chan Kim and Renée Mauborgne, this framework provides a systematic way to make the competition irrelevant by creating a new, uncontested market space (a "blue ocean"). It challenges you to ask four key questions: What factors can we Eliminate that our industry has long competed on? What factors can we Reduce well below the industry standard? What factors can we Raise well above the industry standard? And what factors can we Create that the industry has never offered? A classic example is Cirque du Soleil. Instead of competing with traditional circuses on animal acts and star performers (which they eliminated), they created a new form of entertainment that blended circus arts with theatre, appealing to a whole new audience of adults willing to pay a premium price. They didn't just build a better circus; they redefined what a circus could be. That is the work of the Blue Ocean Strategy.

An innovative organization, therefore, is methodologically omni dextrous. Its leaders and teams are not dogmatically attached to a single process. They may not be masters of every innovation methodology, but they have a deep appreciation for the value of each. They possess the diagnostic wisdom to look at a challenge and ask: "What is the fundamental nature of this problem? Is it a question of empathy, validation, or strategic execution?"

This is the moment of truth where this omni dexterity comes to life. It is the courage to then select the right approach, the wisdom to modify it to fit the unique contours of their business, and the decisiveness to apply it, not as a rigid formula, but as a focused tool to solve the problem at hand.

The Leadership Mandate

But even with motivated people and the right methods, innovation will wither and die if the organization's immune system attacks it as a foreign body. This brings us to the third and most critical layer: the Leadership Mandate. This is not about managing a process; it is about architecting an entire ecosystem where innovation can survive and thrive. It is the leader's highest duty.

This work begins with a profound understanding of the Innovator's Dilemma. As Clayton Christensen demonstrated, the very processes and values that make your core business successful are inherently hostile to disruptive ideas. Therefore, a leader's primary job is to create "safe spaces"—autonomous units shielded from the financial pressures and bureaucratic antibodies of the core business. This is the principle behind legendary innovation cells like Lockheed Martin's "Skunk Works" and Alphabet's moonshot factory, "X." These leaders understood that you cannot grow a sapling in the shadow of a giant oak. You must give it its own patch of sunlight.

However, this act of separation is only half of the mandate. The other, more pervasive duty is to cultivate a universal psychological safety that permeates the core business itself. This is the work of turning the entire organization into fertile ground for everyday innovation. It means creating a culture where a junior engineer can challenge a senior executive's assumption without fear, where a "failed" experiment is treated as a valuable lesson learned, and where every team member feels they have the permission to think like an innovator within their own role. This intrinsic safety doesn't require a separate building or a secret lab; it is built through the daily words and actions of leaders who model curiosity, reward intelligent risk-taking, and protect those who dare to speak a dissenting truth. It architects virtual safe spaces that appear when required, and become dormant when not required, throughout the organization.

This act of separation is part of a broader leadership responsibility: to act as a strategic venture capitalist for the entire enterprise. This means managing a balanced portfolio of bets across different time horizons, a concept powerfully captured in the "Three Horizons" framework. This was first introduced in the book The Alchemy of Growth by McKinsey Consultants, Mehrdad Baghai,

Stephen Coley, and David White. A leader must simultaneously manage the present by optimizing the core business (Horizon 1), build the emerging future by scaling new ventures (Horizon 2), and create options for the distant future by placing small, intelligent bets on radical ideas (Horizon 3).

This is the ultimate act of leadership: running today's business with excellence while simultaneously building the business that will replace it.

These three layers—Drivers, Method, and Management—form a complete, interdependent system. Think of it as the Spark, the Toolbox, and the Greenhouse. The Drivers are the psychological spark of human energy and resilience. The Method is the procedural toolbox of disciplined processes that channels that spark in a productive direction. And Management is the structural greenhouse that protects fragile, emerging ideas from the harsh climate of the core business. An organization that has only one or two of these layers will consistently keep innovation in the shadows. A team with a brilliant Method but no psychological Drivers will lack the energy to start. A team with passionate Drivers but no protective Management will see its best ideas crushed by the corporate immune system. Sustainable innovation only occurs when a leader architects all three layers to function as a single, unified engine. The story of Pixar is a masterclass in conducting this three-part harmony.

The Proof: A Story of Pixels and Pride

In the world of animation, for decades, there was one undisputed king: Disney. From Snow White to The Lion King, Disney's hand-drawn animation was the gold standard, a source of immense pride and a seemingly unassailable artistic and commercial fortress.

In the 1980s, a small group of computer scientists and artists, led by a visionary named Ed Catmull, had a crazy idea. They believed that computers could be used to create a new kind of animation, a three-dimensional world with a depth and realism that hand-drawing could never achieve. This was a disruptive idea in its purest form. The technology was primitive, the process was astronomically expensive, and the results looked cold and lifeless compared to the warm, organic feel of a Disney classic.

This small group, which would eventually become Pixar, was the embodiment of the "Drivers" of innovation. They had a fanatical Grit, working for years in obscurity with little funding. They had a profound Growth Mindset, constantly pushing the boundaries of what was technologically and artistically possible.

After being spun out of Lucasfilm, they were acquired by Steve Jobs, who, despite his own financial struggles at the time, saw the potential and was willing to fund their dream. For years, Pixar survived by making short films and television commercials, all while honing their Method. They developed a unique, iterative process that blended art and technology. They created a culture of radical candour, epitomized by their Braintrust meetings, where directors would present their work-in-progress to a group of their peers and receive brutally honest, constructive feedback. This was their version of the Build-Measure-Learn loop, applied to storytelling.

But their biggest challenge was The Leadership Mandate. They were a tiny, fragile startup trying to create a feature film, an undertaking that cost tens of millions of dollars. They needed a partner. And in a moment of supreme irony, they partnered with the powerhouse they sought to disrupt: Disney.

The relationship was fraught with tension. The Disney executives, masters of the sustaining innovation of 2D animation, were deeply sceptical of Pixar's unproven technology. They imposed creative constraints and demanded changes that clashed with Pixar's vision. This was the classic Innovator's Dilemma in action.

The established giant, focused on protecting its core business, was instinctively trying to crush the disruptive upstart.

The first film born of this partnership was Toy Story. Its production was a near-disaster. At one point, under pressure from Disney to make the story edgier, the main character, Woody, was rewritten to be a sarcastic, unlikable tyrant. When Jobs and the Pixar leadership saw the story reels, they were horrified. They had created a film they didn't believe in.

This was their moment of truth. A less pragmatic team would have pushed forward, caving to the demands of their powerful partner. But Catmull, Jobs, and director John Lasseter made a courageous decision. They halted production. They went back to Disney and, at great personal and financial risk, demanded the chance to rewrite the script from scratch, to make the film they truly wanted to make.

It was an act of profound artistic and strategic courage. They returned to their first principles, focusing on creating characters with heart and a story with genuine emotion. The result was a masterpiece. Toy Story was a global phenomenon. It didn't just make money; it changed an entire industry forever. It proved that computer animation could not only compete with hand-drawn animation but could surpass it in emotional depth and visual splendour.

In 2006, in a stunning reversal of fortune, Disney acquired Pixar for $7.4 billion, and Ed Catmull and John Lasseter were put in charge of all of Disney Animation. The disruptive upstart had effectively taken over the kingdom. The Pixar story is a masterclass in the three layers of innovation. They had the passionate Drivers, they perfected a unique Method, and they had the leadership and courage to protect their vision and manage the hostile Leadership environment until they could prove their case to the world.

The Pixar story is both inspiring and daunting. It perfectly illustrates the power of getting the three layers of innovation right, but it also reveals the immense complexity involved. A leader reading this might reasonably ask: "How can I possibly manage all of this at once? How do I know when my team should be iterating on a story like the Braintrust, versus when they should be optimizing a process? How do I balance running my core business with protecting a disruptive idea?" These are precisely the questions that can lead to paralysis. The story shows us what a complete innovation system looks like; it does not, however, give us a practical tool for managing it day-to-day.

This is why we need a new way of seeing—a simple, powerful frame to help a leader diagnose an innovation challenge and guide their team's response accordingly. This is what we call The Innovator's Lens. It is the conductor's tool for managing the complexities the Pixar story so vividly demonstrates.

The Framework: The Innovator's Lens

A culture of innovation is not a single, monolithic state to be achieved. It is a dynamic capability, a form of organizational omni dexterity. We often see leaders fall into the trap of searching for a single solution to build innovation, a one-size-fits-all solution that simply doesn't exist. A more powerful approach is to cultivate a portfolio of different innovation postures, and with it, the wisdom to know which one is right for the challenge at hand.

For this to happen, a leader will need a new way of seeing. This is what we call The Innovator's Lens.

The Innovator's Lens doesn't give you a bounded solution; it gives you strategic clarity. It's a frame to help you read the innovation challenge accurately and guide your team's response. It works through two integrated parts: The Map, which defines the four distinct fields of play for innovation, and The Postures, the four behavioural modes your team must master to win on each field.

The Map - The Four Fields of Innovation

To create a practical system for innovation, we do not need to invent a new theory from scratch. Instead, we can stand on the shoulders of giants. By synthesizing the foundational work of seminal thinkers like Clayton Christensen, Joseph Schumpeter, and Rebecca Henderson, we can construct a powerful and practical strategic tool: **The Map**.

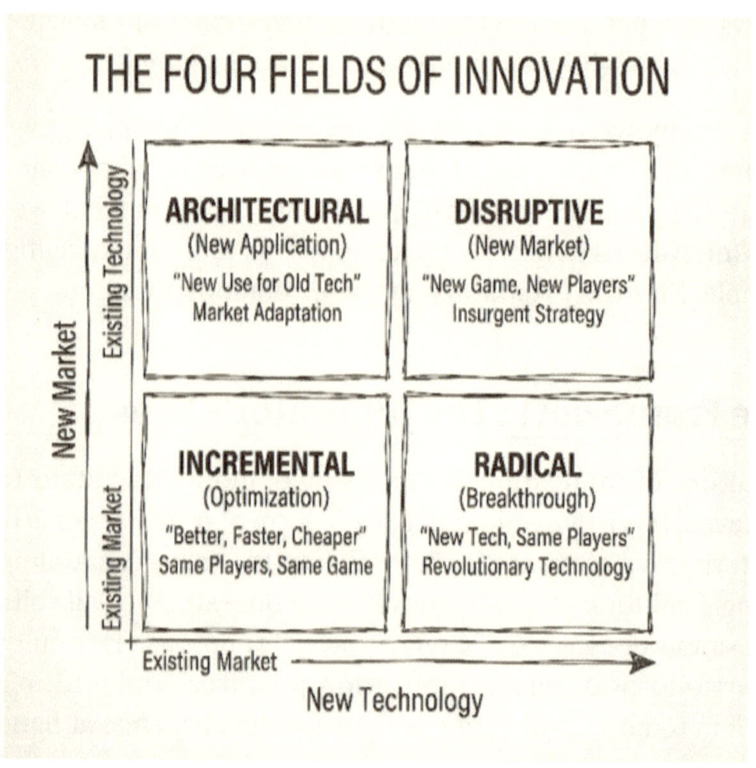

The Four Fields of Innovation

The Innovator's Lens starts with The Map. A leader must first identify which of the four fields they are playing on, as each requires a completely different strategy and team posture.

The Map is a simplified version of a classic strategic matrix, built on two axes: the novelty of the technology being used and the novelty of the market being addressed. Its purpose is to reveal that not all innovation is created equal. By identifying which field an organization is playing on, a leader can move beyond generic advice and deploy a strategy tailored to the specific challenge at hand.

The Incremental Field (Existing Tech, Existing Market) is the home of optimization. Here, the goal is to make your current products better, faster, and cheaper for your current customers. The strategic approach is Operational Excellence, rooted in the principles of Kaizen.

The Radical Field (New Tech, Existing Market) is the realm of the technological breakthrough. Here, you are introducing a revolutionary new technology to your existing market, aiming to render the old way obsolete. The strategic approach is R&D-heavy, a form of Schumpeter's Creative Destruction.

The Architectural Field (Existing Tech, New Market) is the field of clever application. Here, you are taking your existing, proven technology and finding a new market or a new use for it. The strategic approach is Market Adaptation, as described by Henderson & Clark.

The Disruptive Field (New Tech, New Market) is the territory of the insurgent. Here, you are typically using a new, simpler, and more accessible technology to create a brand-new market, often starting with "non-consumers" and then moving up to challenge the incumbents, as so brilliantly diagnosed by Clayton Christensen.

The Postures - How to Win on the Field

Knowing the field is only the first step. To win, a team must adopt the correct behavioural Posture. These are not fixed levels of maturity, but dynamic, context-dependent modes of operating. The power of the Innovator's Lens is in providing your team with the self-awareness to ask, "What posture does this challenge demand of us right now?"

Incremental Field. When playing in the Incremental Field, the required posture is that of The Mechanic. The purpose here is to optimize the existing system, and the team's mantra is a relentless "Make it better". A team in the Mechanic Posture is disciplined, data-driven, and focused on efficiency. They are masters of process improvement, waste reduction, and quality control. This is the healthy, "resting heartbeat" of a well-run operations or manufacturing department. The critical self-awareness indicator for this team is the question: "Are we focused on improving the current process by 10%, or are we trying to invent a new one?" For a Mechanic, a 10% improvement is exactly what winning looks like.

Radical Field. To succeed in the Radical Field, a team must adopt the posture of The Scientist. Their purpose is not to build a finished product, but to validate the feasibility of a new, unproven technology. Their mantra is a constant "Let's test that." A team in the Scientist Posture is experimental, rigorous, and deeply technical. They are comfortable with uncertainty and skilled at designing elegant experiments to answer difficult technical questions. This is the posture of a true R&D team. Their guiding question must always be: "What is the single most critical uncertainty we need to resolve with this experiment?".

Architectural Field. When the challenge lies in the Architectural Field, the team must embody the posture of The Brainstormer. The purpose here is to generate new possibilities and applications, and the mantra is a creative and expansive series of "What ifs...?" A team in the Brainstormer Posture is divergent, empathetic, and skilled at making connections between seemingly unrelated ideas. They excel at imagining new uses for old things, a skill essential for strategy and business development teams looking for new growth areas. Their self-awareness comes from asking: "Are we prematurely judging ideas, or are we creating the space for wild, impractical 'what ifs' that might lead to a breakthrough?"

Disruptive Field. Finally, to compete in the Disruptive Field, a team must adopt the posture of The Insurgent. Their purpose is to create and capture a new, uncontested market, and their mantra is a scrappy "Find a foothold". The Insurgent is a unique blend of Brainstormer and Scientist. They are agile, customer-obsessed, and not trying to build a better version of the incumbent's product. Instead, they are searching for a small, overlooked group of "non-consumers" and building something "good enough" to get started. The self-awareness indicator for an Insurgent team is the crucial question: "Are we trying to compete with the market leader on their terms, or are we trying to find the customers they are ignoring and create a new game?"

The Leader's Role: The Conductor

This brings us to the leader's role. The leader is not meant to live in any single posture. The leader is The Conductor.

A conductor does not play an instrument. A conductor's job is to understand the entire score and to bring out the best in every section of the orchestra at the right time. They know when to call upon the strings for soaring melody (The Brainstormer), when to rely on the precision of the percussion (The Mechanic), and when to feature a complex solo from the woodwinds (The Scientist).

The first step is to Diagnose the Music. With the Innovator's Lens as your guide, you can identify which of the four fields a project truly belongs to. Is the organization playing a gentle waltz of incremental improvement that calls for the precision of a Mechanic? Or is this a radical, disruptive symphony that demands the bold experimentation of a Scientist?

Once you've understood the music, you can Cue the Section. This is about empowering the right team to adopt the right posture for the piece they are playing. It often means giving them explicit permission to behave in a way that feels different from the rest of the organization, protecting them from the corporate immune system that naturally resists the unfamiliar. After all, you wouldn't ask the percussion section to play like the strings and expect a harmonious result.

Finally, the conductor's ultimate role is to ensure harmony across the entire enterprise. This is the art of managing the complete portfolio, ensuring a healthy and vibrant balance of activity across all four fields. Herein lies the essence of the truly agile organization: the ability to conduct the steady, reliable rhythm of the core business while, in parallel, rehearsing the strange and beautiful new music that will become its future; achieving a kinetic stability in sustained growth and readiness for the future.

This is the ultimate act of leadership: not just playing one tune well, but conducting a dynamic and evolving repertoire.

The Call to Action: Becoming the Conductor

The journey to becoming an innovative organization does not begin with a massive budget or a new R&D lab. It begins with a change in perception. It begins with you cleaning off your own lens and learning to see the innovation landscape with new clarity.

Your first task isn't to launch a dozen new projects. It is to take stock of your current ones. Look at your team's existing initiatives and, for each one, ask the two fundamental questions of The Innovator's Lens:

1. What field are we really playing on? (Incremental, Radical, Architectural, or Disruptive?)

2. What posture is our team actually adopting? (Mechanic, Scientist, Brainstormer, or Insurgent?)

The power is in the diagnosis. You may find a team in a "Mechanic" posture trying to tackle a "Disruptive" challenge. This is a recipe for failure. You may find a "Brainstormer" team stuck in an "Incremental" project, leading to frustration and boredom. Your first act as The Conductor is to see this dissonance. Your second is to begin the work of creating harmony—by reassigning the project, reframing the goal, or giving the team the permission to adopt the posture the work truly demands.

Innovation is not a mystery. It is a discipline. It is the discipline of seeing clearly, thinking strategically, and acting with intention. It is the work of a Conductor. The orchestra is waiting. It is time to pick up your baton.

Pocket Summary

- Innovation is a System, Not an Event: Sustainable innovation is not a workshop or a slogan. It is a systemic capability with three layers: the psychological Drivers (Growth Mindset and Grit), the procedural Method (a portfolio of tools like Design Thinking and Lean Startup), and the Leadership Mandate (creating safe spaces and managing a portfolio of bets).

- The Innovator's Dilemma is Real: Well-managed organizations fail because the systems that make them good at optimizing their core business (sustaining innovation) are inherently hostile to the new, uncertain ideas that fuel disruptive innovation.

- Use the Innovator's Lens: To overcome this, a leader needs a new way of seeing. The Innovator's Lens provides this clarity through two parts: The Map and The Postures.

- Diagnose the Field, Adopt the Posture: The Map identifies which of four fields an initiative is on (Incremental, Radical, Architectural, or Disruptive). The Postures define the required team behaviour for each field (Mechanic, Scientist, Brainstormer, or Insurgent). The leader's job is to ensure the team's posture matches the field they are playing on.

Three Questions for Your Team

1. Looking at our most important current project, are we acting more like a Mechanic (optimizing what exists), a Scientist (testing a new technology), a Brainstormer (exploring new uses), or an Insurgent (creating a new market)?

2. Does our current behaviour (our "posture") feel perfectly aligned with the true goal of this project, or is there a mismatch between how we are acting and what we need to achieve?

3. Is there one rule, process, or metric that is making it hardest for us to adopt the posture this specific project truly requires?

Conclusion: From Adaptation to Elevation

The Habit of Innovation, therefore, is the discipline of building a systemic engine for adaptation. It moves an organization beyond the mastery of its current reality and prepares it for the uncertainties of the future. It is the recognition that the blueprint for today's success is a poor guide for tomorrow's survival.

We have seen that this requires a leader to act as an architect of a complete system, one that nurtures the psychological Drivers of creativity, equips teams with a portfolio of Methods, and is protected by a Leadership Mandate that creates safe spaces for new ideas to grow. The core tool for this architectural work is the Innovator's Lens. By using The Map to diagnose the field of play and The Postures to align team behaviour, a leader can move from managing a chaotic series of projects to conducting a harmonious portfolio of innovation. This is the ultimate expression of every organization's dyadic character: the ability to run today's business with ruthless efficiency while simultaneously building the business that will one day replace it.

This brings us to the profound synergy between the habits. Pragmatism gives us a clear view of reality. Empathy reveals the unmet needs and unarticulated desires that are the seeds of opportunity. Engagement unlocks the human energy required to pursue those opportunities. And Innovation provides the system for turning those opportunities into new sources of value.

Yet, even this is not enough. An organization can have a clear plan, a deep understanding of its customers, a highly engaged workforce, and a powerful innovation engine, and still fail. It can fail if the final product is unreliable, if the service is inconsistent, or if the internal processes are riddled with waste. An engine of innovation without a commitment to excellence produces a series of fascinating, but ultimately flawed, prototypes. To ensure that new ideas are not just creative but also robust, and that the core business runs not just efficiently but flawlessly, we need the fifth and final habit. We need a systemic devotion to Quality.

CHAPTER 5

THE HABIT OF QUALITY: THE ARCHITECTURE OF TRUST

Your ship is now a marvel of modern leadership. It is anchored in Pragmatism, seeing reality with unflinching clarity. Its charts are drawn with Empathy, the discipline of understanding the world from the outside-in, through the eyes of your customers and your people. Its sails are filled by the winds of Engagement, the discipline of aligning the entire crew from the inside-out, creating a shared sense of ownership and a unified will to act to align with the ship's true north. And it is equipped with the engine of Innovation, capable of rebuilding itself to adapt to the changing seas.

You have a ship that is clear-eyed, customer-obsessed, unified, and adaptive. By all measures, you should be unstoppable.

But there is one final, insidious threat. It is a threat that can undo all your hard work, sink the most innovative ship, and destroy the most engaged crew. It is the slow, silent corrosion of trust.

Trust is the invisible architecture of your entire enterprise. It is the unspoken faith your customers have that your product will work as promised, every single time. It is the confidence your employees have that the tools they use are reliable and the processes they follow are sound. It is the belief your partners and regulators have that you are an organization that says what it does and does what it says.

This architecture of trust is built on a single, non-negotiable foundation: Quality.

Like the other habits, Quality is a word that has been narrowed and misunderstood. For many, it conjures images of inspectors in white coats at the end of an assembly line, a final, joyless checkpoint designed to catch defects before they escape the factory. This is not Quality. This is merely damage control.

True, strategic Quality is not a final inspection; it is a foundational philosophy. It is not about catching mistakes. It is about building a system where mistakes are difficult to make. It is not a department; it is a pervasive cultural habit of excellence, a shared obsession with reliability, and a deep-seated respect for both the customer who uses the product and the employee who builds it.

If the other habits build a ship that is fast and smart, the Habit of Quality is what makes it seaworthy. It is what ensures that when you promise your customers a safe and reliable journey, you deliver on that promise, every single time.

The Character of Quality

In the architecture of any great organization, the final and perhaps most crucial structural element is its definition of Quality. This is more than a process or a department; it is a declaration of character. It reveals an organization's deepest assumptions about responsibility, and its answer to a single, profound question: What does it mean for our work to be "good"?

The traditional answer, rooted in the philosophy of Quality Control (QC), is that good means free of defects. This gives rise to a reactive posture of inspection and firefighting, a system designed to catch failures before they escape. A more evolved answer, born from the Quality Assurance (QA) movement and the foundational work of W. Edwards Deming, is that "good" means the whole process is good. This shifts the posture to proactive prevention, focusing on designing the system to eliminate the conditions for failure. Deming's core insight, that the system, not the individual, is the source of most failures, was a revolutionary step forward.

But today, even this is not enough. The most durable and respected organizations have pushed this evolution further, expanding their definition of "good" beyond the product and the process to encompass the entire ecosystem in which they operate. This modern character of quality is defined by two principles: radical ownership and a relentlessly proactive posture.

This expanded form of ownership means taking responsibility for the entire lifecycle and impact of a product. Internally, it means owning the quality of the work experience itself. Externally, it extends beyond the functional to the ethical and empathetic. It means owning compliance with cultural and regulatory requirements as a baseline promise to society. More profoundly, it means owning the empathetic requirements of the customer, such as a commitment to sustainability, ethical sourcing, and responsible manufacturing. The posture, therefore, must also evolve. It becomes a proactive stewardship of this entire ecosystem; auditing suppliers for ethical practices, designing products for longevity and repair, and taking responsibility for a product even after it has been sold.

Perhaps no company embodies this modern character of quality more completely than the outdoor apparel company Patagonia. For Patagonia, a jacket is not a quality product simply because its seams are well-stitched. Its quality is a function of its entire ecosystem. This is demonstrated in their "Worn Wear" program, which actively encourages customers to repair their gear instead of replacing it, and even provides a marketplace for used items. This is a radical act of ownership, extending responsibility for the product's lifespan far beyond the point of sale and directly challenging the consumerist model of planned obsolescence.

Furthermore, their fanatical commitment to supply chain transparency and environmental standards is not a marketing initiative; it is a core function of their quality assurance. They invest heavily in auditing suppliers for fair labour practices and environmental impact, making this data public. This proactive posture assumes that a product's quality is inseparable from the ethics of its creation. For Patagonia, a defect is not just a broken zipper; a defect is a polluted river, an exploited worker, or a jacket that ends up in a landfill prematurely. Their success proves that this expanded definition of quality is not just a moral stance, but a powerful and profitable strategic position. They have built an entire brand on the character of a quality ecosystem.

The Proof: The Two Sides of a Vial

The race for the COVID-19 vaccine provides one of the most powerful and revealing case studies of a modern quality character—both in its strengths and its limitations. The effort by the American pharmaceutical giant Pfizer and the German biotech firm BioNTech to produce billions of doses of a revolutionary mRNA vaccine, in record time, was a masterclass in operational quality.

In the face of a global crisis, their quality character was forged around two core principles. First, they demonstrated an excellent form of Systemic Ownership over the technical process. They understood that quality was not the responsibility of any single supplier but their own, end-to-end. They built a unified, digital control tower for real-time visibility across a supply chain involving 86 suppliers in 19 countries. Custom-built shipping containers with GPS and thermal sensors didn't just track vials; they guaranteed their integrity. Ownership was not a person; it was an architecture.

Second, they adopted a relentlessly proactive posture to prevent failure. To scale production, they embarked on a massive copy and paste effort, meticulously replicating the exact same production lines and equipment in facilities across the US and Europe. They then flew their most experienced engineers between sites to transfer not just process documents, but deep, tacit knowledge. This was a fanatical devotion to eliminating process variation, ensuring a vial produced in Michigan was, at a molecular level, indistinguishable from one produced in Belgium. This operational execution was a triumph of the principles established by Deming and Toyota, applied at unprecedented speed and scale.

However, the story also reveals the limits of a quality definition that is not fully expanded to the entire ecosystem. While Pfizer and BioNTech achieved near-perfect process quality, they faced significant criticism on the grounds of access quality. The initial distribution of the vaccine was heavily skewed towards wealthy nations that could afford to place large advance orders, leaving many poorer countries waiting for months. From a purely operational perspective, this was rational; they were fulfilling contracts. From the perspective of a broader quality ecosystem, one that defines ownership by the ultimate success of all potential end-users, this outcome represented a different set of priorities and trade-offs.

This is not to diminish the monumental technical achievement. Rather, it is to use it as a lens to examine the strategic choices inherent in defining a quality character. The posture adopted by Pfizer and BioNTech was one of flawless execution within the boundaries of their contractual and logistical system; a masterclass in process integrity.

An alternative posture, one based on a broader definition of the quality ecosystem, might have prioritized global access alongside process control, potentially involving different partnership models, tiered pricing, or proactive technology transfers from the outset. The Pfizer/BioNTech story is the definitive narrative of modern operational quality executed under extreme pressure. It also serves as a powerful illustration that the boundaries an organization draws around its ecosystem, and the posture it chooses to adopt within it, are among the most consequential strategic decisions a leader can make.

The Framework: The Five Characters of Quality Maturity

An organization's relationship with quality is a direct reflection of its character. It evolves from a state of reactive blame to one of proactive, systemic excellence.

The Finger Pointer - The Blame Organization. At the lowest level is The Finger-Pointer. This is the Level 1 Blame Organization. Its character is toxic and fearful. When a mistake occurs, the immediate, instinctive reaction is not "What went wrong?" but "Who is to blame?". Failure is a source of shame and punishment. As a result, mistakes are hidden, data is manipulated, and problems are allowed to fester beneath the surface until they become catastrophic. There is no psychological safety, and therefore, no learning.

The Fire fighter – The Reactive Organization. This is the next level. The Firefighter's character is one of heroic chaos. This organization doesn't necessarily blame individuals, but it is trapped in a cycle of constant crisis. It lurches from one urgent problem to the next, celebrating the "heroes" who stay late to fix the latest self-inflicted disaster. Because it is always focused on fighting the fire (the symptom), it never has the time or energy to investigate the faulty wiring (the root cause). The same problems recur, predictably.

The Problem Solver – The Accountable Organization. The first step toward true quality is becoming The Problem-Solver. This is the Level 3 Accountable Organization. The Problem-

Solver's character is responsible. When a problem occurs, this organization takes ownership. The first question is not "Who?" but "Why?". It uses simple but powerful tools like the "5 Whys" analysis, popularized by Toyota, to dig down to the root cause of an issue. The Problem-Solver is good at fixing problems so they stay fixed.

The Architect – The proactive Organization. A higher level of maturity is found in The Architect. This is the Level 4 Proactive Organization. The Architect's character is one of intentional design. This organization is no longer content to just solve problems as they arise; it seeks to prevent them from ever happening. It has fully embraced the philosophy of Quality Assurance. It designs its processes, its systems, and its products with the explicit goal of making it easy to do things right and difficult to do them wrong. It uses tools like checklists, standardized work, and mistake-proofing to build quality into the system from the very beginning.

The Black Box Thinker – The High Reliability Organization. Finally, at the pinnacle, is The Black Box Thinker. This is the Level 5 High-Reliability Organization. Its character is one of enlightened learning. This organization has achieved a state of profound psychological safety. It understands the complex space in which it operates, and has achieved highly reliable systems where failure is rare. It does not however believe that failure will not happen. But it also understands that failure is the most valuable source of data for improvement. It treats every failure, every near-miss, every anomaly with the same rigor that the aviation industry treats a plane crash. The goal is not to assign blame, but to extract the maximum possible learning to make the entire system smarter, safer, and more resilient. The Black Box Thinker does not just tolerate failure; it learns from it more effectively than its competitors.

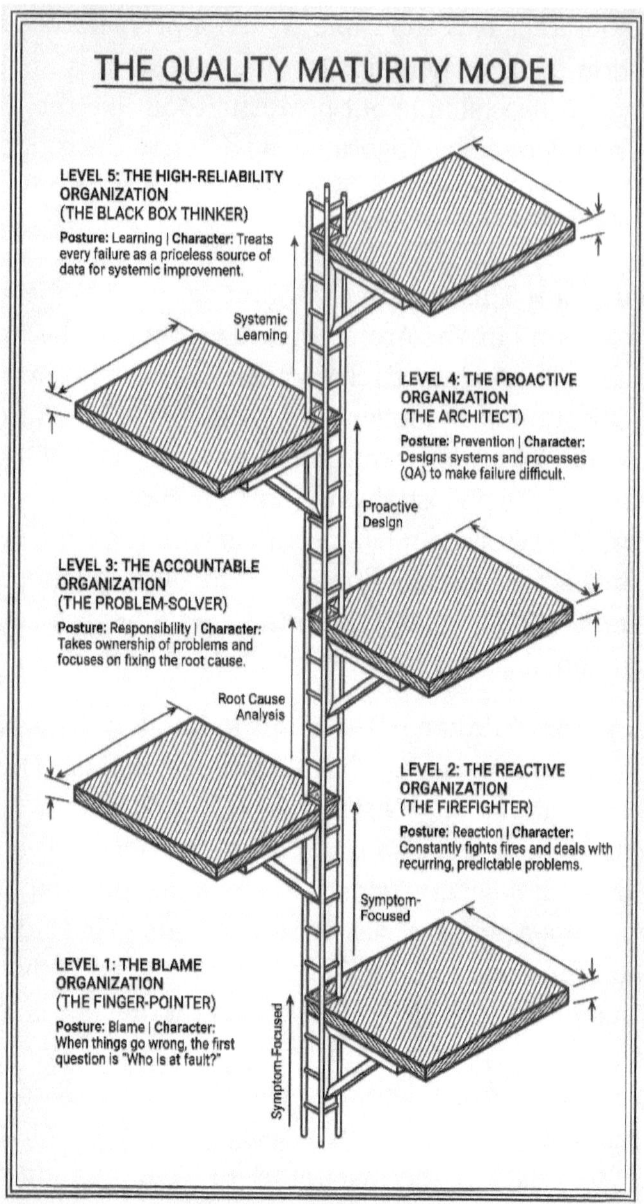

The journey to Quality is a five-level evolution of organizational character, from the toxic Finger-Pointer to the enlightened Black Box Thinker.

The Call to Action: Your First Act of Quality

You cannot create a culture of quality with a memo. You must demonstrate it with your actions. You must show your people that you are more interested in fixing the system than in blaming the individual.

Your first act of Quality is to change your response to the next mistake. The next time a team member comes to you to report a problem, a missed deadline, a customer complaint, a flawed piece of code, resist the powerful, instinctive urge to ask "Why did you do that?".

Instead, take a deep breath, and respond with a different narrative: "Lets work together to find out what went wrong. What can we learn from this?" And then, most importantly, ask, "What was it about our systems and assumptions that made it easy for this mistake to happen?"

This simple shift in language is a revolutionary act. It depersonalizes the failure and focuses the team on the system. It is a clear signal that you are a leader who hunts for bad processes, not bad people. It is the first, essential step in building an architecture of trust.

Pocket Summary

- **Quality is Character.** An organization›s character is revealed by how it defines quality. This has evolved from reactive Quality Control (catching defects) to proactive Quality Assurance (preventing defects by improving the system), a shift pioneered by W. Edwards Deming.

- **Define Your Ecosystem.** The most advanced form of quality requires expanding ownership beyond the product to the entire ecosystem. This includes the internal work experience, regulatory compliance, and the empathetic and ethical values of your customers (such as sustainability or fair labour practices).

- **Ownership and Posture are Strategic Choices.** Ownership defines the boundaries of your responsibility—from the product, to the process, to the entire ecosystem. Your Posture is either reactive (firefighting problems) or proactive (designing the system to prevent them).

- **There Are Trade-offs.** As the Pfizer/BioNTech case illustrates, it is possible to achieve world-class operational quality within a defined system. However, a broader ecosystem view might lead to different strategic priorities and outcomes. The key leadership act is to consciously decide how wide to draw the circle of ownership.

Three Questions for Your Team

1. Which would we consider a more significant quality failure: a 1% defect rate in our shipped product, or the discovery that a key supplier in our chain uses unethical labour practices?

2. Beyond the functional performance of our product/service, what are the most important ethical or empathetic requirements of our customers (e.g., sustainability, privacy, accessibility), and are we measuring our quality against those standards?

3. If we had to draw a line defining the boundary of our quality ecosystem, where would we draw it today? Does it end when the product ships, when the customer is successful, or when our product's lifecycle is complete?

Conclusion: The Character of the Architect

The Habit of Quality, in its highest form, is therefore not a set of processes, but a conscious and deliberate choice of character. It is the final, load-bearing pillar of the EPIQUE framework, ensuring that the entire structure is not just elegantly designed but is also sound, durable, and worthy of trust.

We have seen that this character is defined by an organization's answers to two questions: how broadly it defines its Ownership and how deliberately it chooses its Posture. The journey from a reactive posture of inspection to a proactive posture of prevention is a crucial step. But the ultimate evolution is the expansion of ownership—from the product, to the process, and finally to the entire ecosystem. This means taking responsibility not just for the thing you make, but for the experience of those who make it, the success of those who use it, and the impact it has on the world. As the story of the COVID-19 vaccine illustrates, where a leader chooses to draw the boundaries of this ecosystem is one of the most consequential strategic decisions they can make.

This brings us to the ultimate synthesis of the five habits. Pragmatism provides a foundation in reality. Empathy connects us to the human needs within the ecosystem. Engagement channels the energy to serve those needs. Innovation provides the engine to remain relevant for tomorrow. And Quality is the commitment that ensures the work is done with integrity, responsibility, and excellence.

Separately, they are powerful disciplines. Together, they form a single, coherent system for building an organization that is not just successful, but is also resilient, respected, and built to last.

Now, it is time to step back and look at the complete blueprint.

PART 2

THE ARCHITECT IN ACTION

CHAPTER 6

ORCHESTRATING THE EPIQUE CONVERSATION

The Conductor's Silence

Imagine a world-class orchestra, moments before a performance. The musicians are virtuosos, their instruments priceless. The audience waits in hushed anticipation. The conductor walks to the podium, raises his baton, and in that electric silence, they do not make a sound. Instead, they listen. They listen for the cough in the audience, the rustle of a program, the almost imperceptible hum of the concert hall's lights. They are absorbing the full reality of the environment before they even begin to fill it.

This is the first, most misunderstood secret of great leadership. We know that a leader's job is to have the vision, to give the speech, to set the direction—to make the music. But the greatest leaders, like the greatest conductors, understand that their primary and most powerful act is not to transmit, but to receive. Their first job is to listen, not just to the notes on the page, but to the sound of the room.

This chapter is about the leader's most important instrument: the conversation. It is not about learning to give better speeches. It is about learning to architect a constellation of rich conversations.

It is about trading the megaphone for a tuning fork and learning to use your conductor's baton not just to direct, but to invite, to question, and to orchestrate. It is about transforming the cacophony of daily corporate communication into a powerful, coherent symphony.

The Shift: From Running the Loop to Mastering the Rhythm

The defining challenge of modern leadership is not a lack of information, but a surplus of complexity. The environment is no longer a predictable landscape to be mapped, but a volatile sea of constant, unpredictable change. This is the shift from a VUCA to a BANI reality, where the world is not just complex but often truly incomprehensible, and where cause and effect have become dangerously non-linear. In this reality, the strategic imperative is not just speed, but the velocity of adaptation. The organization that can observe reality more clearly, orient to it more quickly, and act on it more decisively than its competition will invariably own the future.

Many of the most effective leaders have converged on a powerful mental model for this task, a framework forged not in business school, but in the high-stakes world of aerial combat. Developed by military strategist Colonel John Boyd, the Observe, Orient, Decide, Act or OODA loop is the battle-tested operating system for decision-making in dynamic environments. Boyd's insight was that victory belongs to the pilot who can cycle through this loop faster and more effectively than their opponent. The same is true for organizations.

This is the current reality of high-performance leadership: running the loop. But while the OODA loop is a brilliant and enduring model, it is but the frame. Boyd himself considered the "Orient" phase a complex synthesis of culture, experience, and analysis, but in practice, the model doesn't prescribe how a large organization can achieve this shared orientation. It provides the what, but the how is often left to intuition or is addressed with fragmented, domain-specific tools. The loop tells you that you need an engine, but it does not give you the engine itself.

This is where a critical performance gap exists. An organization can run the loop with a sputtering, inefficient engine, burning enormous energy for very little forward momentum. The decisive edge comes from executing each stage with superior quality. It means Observing not just market data, but the deep, unarticulated truths of human need. It means Orienting not just a team, but an entire ecosystem around a shared understanding. It means ensuring Decisions are not merely made, but are deeply committed to by a fully engaged organization. And it means ensuring Actions are not just reactions, but are disciplined acts of innovation.

The EPIQUE framework is the high-performance engine designed to be installed within the OODA loop. It is a coherent system for supercharging each OODA cycle, transforming it from a simple process into a powerful, rhythmic cadence of elite performance. It provides the integrated "how" for each "what", turning the cycle from a frantic reaction into a masterful orchestration. The goal is no longer just to be ahead of the curve. It is to be the one who is drawing it.

Orchestrating the Loop: An Architectural Blueprint

Installing the EPIQUE framework within the OODA loop transforms leadership from a passive cycle into a deliberate act of organizational drive. It provides the architectural blueprint for mastering each stage of the loop with intention and precision. What follows is a guide to how a leader, acting as the architect of this high-performance system, orchestrates this powerful new rhythm.

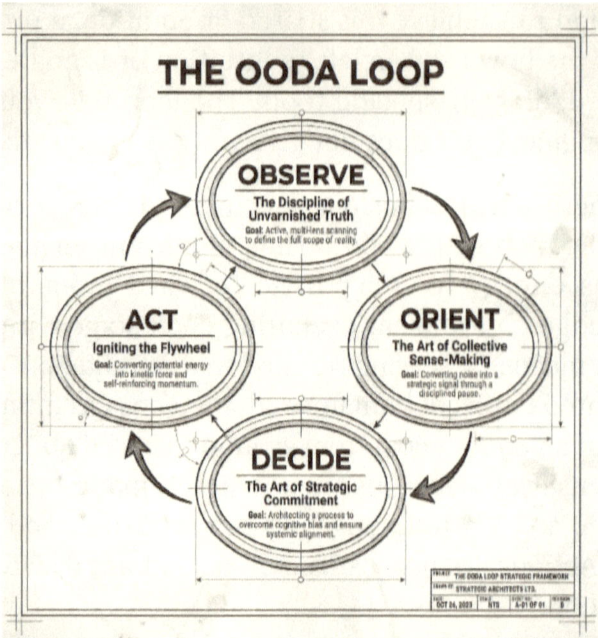

Observe: The Discipline of Unvarnished Truth.

The OODA loop begins with Observation. For a fighter pilot, it is the blip on the radar. For a leader, it is the quarterly sales data. But a leader who only looks at these formal instruments is missing most of the picture. True observation is not a passive act of receiving reports; it is an active, disciplined hunt for the complete truth, conducted with the rigor of a master strategist.

Before you can make sense of reality (Orient), you must first define the full scope of reality worth seeing. Blind spots are not born from a failure of analysis. They are born from a failure of attention; a failure to even cast your gaze in the right direction. The first duty of the leader in the Observe phase is therefore to apply a structured, multi-lens approach to scanning the environment, drawing from decades of strategic thought. This is not a single glance, but a deliberate continuous and ongoing, survey across three distinct domains:

The Macro-Environment (The Distant Weather). First, the

leader must look far beyond their own industry to understand the broad forces shaping the world. A common starting point for this is the PESTLE analysis, a framework for scanning the Political, Economic, Sociocultural, Technological, Legal, and Environmental currents. While useful for initial brainstorming, its classic application often produces a simple list of factors, which can overlook the critical interdependencies between them; how a technological shift, for instance, creates profound social and economic shockwaves. The architectural leader, therefore, uses PESTLE as a tool for initial data collection. The subsequent, more critical work is to move beyond the list and map these forces as a dynamic system, identifying the causal loops and feedback mechanisms that reveal the underlying structure of the emerging reality.

The Competitive Arena (The Field of Play). Next, the leader zooms in on the specific industry. The classic framework for this remains Michael E. Porter's powerful Five Forces model. This assesses the competitive landscape by analysing the threat of new entrants, the power of suppliers and buyers, the danger of substitutes, and the intensity of rivalry. However, applying this 1979 model without a modern lens can be misleading. It provides a static snapshot of a well-defined industry. By focusing on adversarial relationships, one can overlook the immense value created through partnerships. Recognizing this, strategists Adam Brandenburger and Barry Nalebuff, in their work on "Co-opetition," effectively proposed what could be considered a sixth force: the power of Complementors. These are businesses whose products or services make yours more valuable. Including complementors in the analysis provides a more complete strategic picture, shifting the perspective from a purely zero-sum view of competition to a more realistic mix of competition and cooperation.

The Internal Reality (The State of Your Ship). Finally, the leader must turn the lens inward with unsentimental honesty. A common starting point is the SWOT analysis, but its value is often limited to a simple brainstorming of perceived strengths. A list of strengths is not the same as a strategy. To truly understand your capabilities, you must move beyond a simple inventory and begin a more rigorous strategic audit. A powerful framework for this is the VRIO model (Valuable, Rare, Imitable, Organization), developed by strategist Jay B. Barney. It provides a systematic way to assess whether a resource or capability is a true source of sustainable competitive advantage. It guides a leader through a series of cascading questions: Is this capability truly Valuable in the market? Is it Rare among our competitors? Is it difficult or costly to Imitate? And, most critically, is our organization actually structured to exploit it? Only a capability that meets all four criteria can be considered a source of durable strength. This analysis provides a clear-eyed distinction between true strategic assets and capabilities that are merely the cost of doing business.

By applying these three lenses—from the macro-environment to the competitive arena to the internal reality—a leader moves beyond passive monitoring. You are no longer just seeing the world; you are actively building a rich, multi-layered, and evidence-based model of it.

Orient: The Art of Collective Sense-Making

Observation provides the raw inputs; the facts, figures, and stories. But information without interpretation is merely noise. The Orient phase is where leadership creates its most profound value. It is the deliberate act of turning the chaotic noise of the real world into a coherent strategic signal. While many teams are skilled at gathering information and are quick to jump to action, the discipline of pausing to collectively make sense of that information is the pivot that separates reactive teams from truly adaptive ones. This disciplined pause is the very essence of Collective Sense-Making.

This is not a complex process. It is a sequence of inquiry; a conversational habit that a leader can cultivate until it becomes second nature. It is a mental model for guiding any conversation, from a formal project review to an impromptu hallway discussion, to a deeper level of clarity. This model follows the natural logic of the EPIQUE compass.

You begin by anchoring the conversation in Pragmatism, the discipline of seeing reality. Before any opinions, solutions, or strategies are discussed, you must first establish the unvarnished truth. The most powerful questions a leader can ask to cut through corporate politeness and get to the heart of the matter is: "What is the brutal truth here? What are we all pretending not to know? Do you need any other things from me?" These questions give the team permission to be intellectually honest. It creates a safe space to name the elephant in the room, whether it's a missed sales number, a failing project, or a toxic team dynamic. Until the truth is on the table, any further conversation is just a fantasy.

A fact, however, is sterile until its impact is interpreted, understood and contextualized. Therefore, the moment of Pragmatic observation immediately engages the habit of Systemic Empathy. This is the architectural work of mapping the emotional, political, and structural landscape surrounding the truth that has been uncovered. The guiding question moves from "What is true?" to "Who is affected by this truth, and what does the world look like from their position?" This is not an exercise in sentiment, but in strategic analysis. It involves applying the three lenses of empathy to understand what this truth means for the customer, the frontline employee, the investor, and the regulator. It is the discipline of understanding their unique "Job to be Done", their likely perceptions, and their probable behaviours, thereby providing critical intelligence that prevents a technically sound plan from being derailed by stakeholder reality.

With a clear map of the external and internal viewpoints, you then turn to Engagement, the discipline of creating a shared path forward. This is where you connect the problem to your internal and external stakeholder's purpose, and begin the process of co-creating a solution. This is not about dictating a plan; it is about initiating genuine conversations. The essential question to spark this is: "Given this reality and these viewpoints, how can we move forward together?". This question is an invitation. It signals a shift from "I have a plan" to "Let's build a plan". It's an opportunity to soft-sell an initial idea, gather and honour, in a pragmatic manner, honest feedback, and forge the idea for robustness and buy-in. This will form the foundation of true commitment from your stakeholders.

This dialogue naturally leads to Innovation, the discipline of exploring new possibilities. As the team discusses how to move forward, the leader's role is to challenge the default path of simply trying harder. The Conductor must ask the question that forces a strategic choice: "Does this situation call for a better version of our current game, or do we need to invent a new one?". This question opens the door to a richer conversation. It encourages the team to consider if the solution is a simple process improvement (a Mechanic's job) or if it requires a more radical rethinking of the entire approach (the work of a Scientist or Insurgent). The goal here is not to generate final solutions, but to define the strategic arena in which the team will compete. This choice of 'which game to play' is the critical output of the Orient phase and the primary input for the Decide phase.

Finally, as your options begin to form (and not later), you must apply the lens of Quality, the discipline of building for resilience. This is the proactive habit of anticipating and preventing failure. Before the meeting ends and the action begins, the leader must ask the forward-looking question: "What is the most likely point of failure in this plan, and how can we design a system to prevent it?". This question shifts the team's mindset from optimistic execution to rigorous, pre-mortem thinking. It is the work of identifying the weakest link in the chain and mistake-proofing it before it has a chance to break. It is the final, essential step that ensures a brilliant strategy is also a robust one.

Orientation is a deeply collaborative act. This is the essence of orchestration: the leader bringing different sections together not just to play the notes, but to collectively interpret the music. It is a structured conversation where the goal is not to win a debate, but to arrive at the richest, most accurate possible understanding of reality, and the options on the table.

Decide: The Art of Strategic Commitment

Once the team has achieved a shared orientation to reality and has chosen a broad strategic direction (e.g., "we need to invent a new game"), and acknowledged the options within this direction, the next step is to Decide. This is where the divergent exploration of the Orient phase becomes the convergent focus of the Decide phase. It is the moment of commitment, where a general direction is translated into a specific, executable plan. In a complex organization, this is not about a single, heroic leader making a snap judgment. It is about architecting a process that overcomes our natural biases and leads to a robust, executable choice.

The most common and insidious failure in decision-making is not choosing the wrong option, but making what appears to be the right one in isolation; a decision that is fractured from the whole. Isolated solutions create a cascade of new problems. This is a core principle of Systems Thinking, as articulated by Peter Senge in The Fifth Discipline.

To prevent this, the leader must architect a process that transforms a mere choice into a well-founded commitment. This is achieved by testing any proposed decision against decades of research into how great decisions are actually made, and how they go wrong; specifically the works of Nobel laureate Daniel Kahneman on cognitive bias and the practical decision-making frameworks of Chip and Dan Heath. There are three sound disciplines for this.

The Discipline of Alternatives. This is the first leg of the tripod. Decision expert Paul Nutt, analyzed over 400 major organizational decisions and found that teams who considered only one option (a "whether or not" choice) failed a staggering 52% of the time. In contrast, those who considered at least one other viable alternative saw their failure rate drop to 32%. The leader's first job in the Decide phase, therefore, is to fight what the Heath brothers, in their book, Decisive, call the narrow frame bias. You must insist on genuine options within the chosen strategic direction. The essential question here is not 'what should we do?' but rather: 'Now that we know our direction, what are two or three distinct and viable ways we could execute it?' This simple act of generating concrete execution plans short-circuits our confirmation bias and dramatically improves the quality of the final choice.

The Discipline of Inquiry. Once alternatives are on the table, you must test the assumptions upon which they are built. As Nobel laureate Daniel Kahneman explains in his masterpiece, Thinking, Fast and Slow, our minds are wired to jump to conclusions based on limited information. The discipline of inquiry is the deliberate act of slowing down to "think slow", to actively seek out disconfirming evidence. The guiding question here is: "What would have to be true for this option to be the right answer, and how can we test that assumption?". This forces the team to move from advocacy to inquiry, from arguing for their preferred option to stress-testing the critical assumptions behind all of them.

The Discipline of Consequences. The third and final leg of the tripod recognizes that a decision is not a single event but the start of a chain reaction within a complex system. This discipline involves applying the principles of Systems Thinking not to predict the future, but to diagnose the nature of the system we are about to change. It helps us understand the existing feedback loops and interconnections. Armed with this systemic understanding, the team can then conduct a forward-looking premortem. This involves asking the critical question: "Imagine it is six months from now, and this decision has failed catastrophically. What could have caused that failure?". This exercise forces the team to think through potential unintended consequences and second-order effects, ensuring the chosen path is not just attractive now, but is also resilient to the complex realities of the system it is about to enter.

A decision that has been forged through this process, one that arose from genuine alternatives, was tested by rigorous inquiry, and whose consequences have been carefully considered, is not just a choice; it is a strategic commitment. It is a clear, unambiguous, and powerful keynote. It is a note that every section of the orchestra can understand, believe in, and play with conviction.

Act: Igniting the Flywheel

The OODA loop culminates in Action. This is the moment where the vast potential energy, built through the rigorous work of Observation, Orientation, and Decision-making, is converted into kinetic force. The organization has achieved a rare state: it possesses a clear, evidence-based view of reality, a deep empathetic and strategic orientation, and a resilient, well-founded commitment to a chosen path. Even though the potential consequences have been anticipated and a robust plan is in place, this is also the moment where the intended impact of many well-architected strategies begins to dissipate.

They collide with the immense inertia of the existing organization, the whirlwind of daily urgencies that consumes all energy and resists any deviation from the norm. A leader who has brought their team this far cannot afford to let this hard-won potential diffuse in a single, fleeting burst of activity. The goal is not to create a momentary push for change. The goal is to use the clarity and commitment from the OOD stages to ignite a self-reinforcing momentum of the OODA flywheel.

The flywheel, a concept masterfully detailed by Jim Collins in his book Good to Great, is a heavy wheel that takes immense effort to get moving. The first few pushes are slow and grinding. But as consistent effort is applied, the wheel begins to turn faster. Each push builds on the work of the last, and soon, the momentum becomes self-reinforcing. The flywheel's own weight begins to work for you, creating unstoppable progress that is no longer dependent on heroic effort.

To make a decision stick, leaders must act to build this flywheel of momentum on three distinct levels simultaneously: the individual, the team, and the organization.

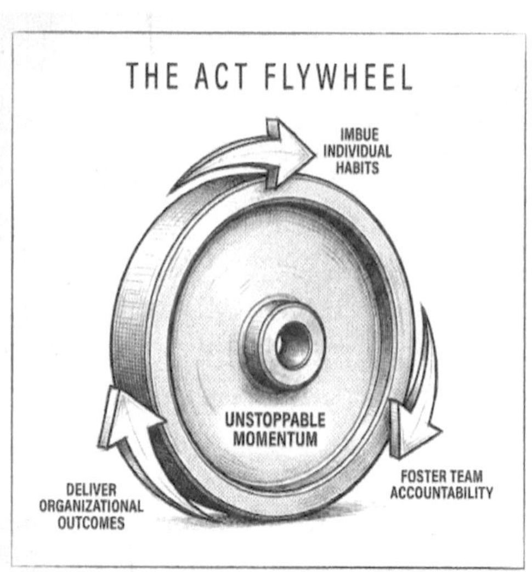

At the Individual level, the aim is to **Imbue Habits**. A new strategy is just a fantasy until it changes the daily behaviour of individuals. This principle is at the heart of the work on habit formation, most powerfully articulated by James Clear in his book Atomic Habits. Clear argues that profound change comes from the accumulation of small, consistent actions. The leader's job, therefore, is to act as a habit architect, designing and coaching the small, daily routines that will make the new way of working the default. This is the work of translating a grand strategic decision into the atomic habits of the front line.

At the second tier is **The Team**. The idea here is to Create Mutual Accountability. Once individuals begin to adopt new habits, the focus must shift to team dynamics. As Patrick Lencioni demonstrated in his seminal work, The Five Dysfunctions of a Team, the most effective teams are not those where the leader holds everyone accountable. They are the ones where peers hold each other accountable to the standards and decisions they have collectively committed to. The leader's action here is to foster this culture of peer-to-peer accountability. This is done by creating clarity on commitments and then facilitating the difficult but essential conversations that must happen when those commitments are not met.

The third and highest level is to **Deliver Outcomes**. This is about focusing the entire organizational system on the path you've set for yourself. The Four Disciplines of Execution framework, developed by McChesney, Covey, and Huling, provides a powerful blueprint for this. Their research shows that to overcome the whirlwind of daily urgencies; leaders must act to focus the organization on a "wildly important goal". This involves identifying and relentlessly tracking the lead measures, the high-leverage activities that drive the outcome, and maintaining a compelling scoreboard that is visible to everyone. The leader's action here is to keep the organization focused on the activities that will actually deliver the promised outcome, not just on being busy.

Action, therefore, is a complete system. It begins with shaping the habits of the individual, is reinforced by the accountability of the team, and is directed by the focus of the entire organization. This is how a single decision is transformed into unstoppable momentum.

The Master Process: The Meta-Flywheel

The execution flywheel within the "Act" phase is powerful; it builds momentum for a single, committed decision. But the true genius of the OODA loop is revealed when we zoom out to see the entire cycle as a higher-order process: **The Meta-Flywheel**.

This is the strategic flywheel that feeds, directs, and learns from the execution flywheel. It is the engine of adaptation that ensures the organization is not just acting, but acting on the right things, at the right time.

Each complete turn of the Observe-Orient-Decide-Act cycle is a single push on this execution flywheel. The first turn is always the hardest. The observation is clumsy; the orientation is slow. But the feedback from that first action immediately informs the next observation, making the second loop faster and smarter. As an organization internalizes this rhythm, a profound transformation occurs. Observation becomes more acute as peripheral vision improves; Orientation becomes more intuitive as the team develops shared mental models; Decision-making grows quicker and more confident; and Action becomes more aligned and impactful. The next OODA cycle forms, and the cycle continues.

This is how an organization builds adaptive momentum; this is the Meta Flywheel, of decisions after decisions. The speed and voracity of its Meta-Flywheel is its single greatest competitive advantage. It is no longer just executing a plan; it is developing a masterful, reflexive capability to see reality, make sense of it, and act decisively, over and over again, with increasing speed and grace. This is the ultimate goal of the Conductor: not just to lead a single performance, but to build an orchestra that can learn any piece of music faster and better than any other in the world.

The Rehearsal: The Conductor's Inner Dialogue

Before a conductor ever steps onto the podium, they have already led the orchestra a hundred times in their mind. They have discussed the score at meetings, studied the score, anticipated the difficult passages, and felt the swell of the crescendo. This is not mere daydreaming; it is a highly disciplined cognitive technique. The physical rehearsal is merely the final confirmation of a performance that has already been perfected internally.

This is the final and most crucial skill of the EPIQUE Conductor. This practice of mental rehearsal, or running internal simulations, is one of the most consistent differentiators between novice and expert performers in every field. Research in cognitive science, famously synthesized by thinkers like Daniel Kahneman, shows that experts build sophisticated mental models of their environment. They use these models to run complex simulations, allowing them to see possibilities that others miss. Elite athletes use visualization to pre-play a perfect performance, wiring their brains and bodies for success long before the game begins.

For a leader, this inner rehearsal is a form of strategic wargaming. It is the discipline of stress-testing their own thinking before entering a high-stakes meeting or conversation. This structured internal dialogue uses the EPIQUE framework not as a checklist, but as a guide for rigorous self-interrogation.

The process begins with Pragmatism: you lay out the objective facts of the situation, separating evidence from assumption. Next, you use Empathy to mentally walk in the shoes of the other key players, asking, "What does this situation look like from their perspective? What are their pressures and priorities?" With this understanding, you can anticipate points of friction and resistance (Engagement). You then challenge your own preferred outcome with Innovation, asking, "Is there a different, better way to achieve our goal?" Finally, you apply the lens of Quality, running what psychologist Gary Klein calls a premortem; imagining the conversation has already failed and asking "Why?". This helps identify the weakest links in your logic and prepares you for the most likely objections.

Based on this internal simulation, you Decide on your opening tempo, not a final answer, but a robust starting hypothesis for the conversation. Finally, you Act by stepping onto the podium to initiate the real-world OODA loop with your team. You are not walking in cold; you have already navigated the most likely paths and pressure-tested your assumptions.

This mental rehearsal is the source of the conductor's seemingly effortless grace under pressure. As the real conversation unfolds, you are constantly running micro-loops in your head; observing, re-orienting, and deciding on the next question. This is the deep, internal work that allows you to lead at a higher cadence, transforming the chaos of organizational life into a coherent and resonant performance.

Shaping high stakes Engagements

An expert leader does not walk into a high-stakes meeting hoping for a good outcome. Instead, they have already achieved this outcome dozens of times in their mind. This is the discipline of strategic rehearsal, a form of cognitive wargaming that consistently separates elite performers from novices in every field. It is not about memorizing a script. It is about stress-testing a strategy before it makes contact with reality.

The rehearsal is a structured, internal dialogue guided by the five habits of the EPIQUE framework. It begins with Pragmatism: the leader lays out the unshakeable facts of the situation, ruthlessly separating evidence from assumption. Next comes Empathy, where the leader mentally crosses the table and asks, "What does this situation look like from their side? What are their pressures, their priorities, their fears?". The ideas of innovation, engagement and quality, serve to shape the potential way forward for the issues at hand.

This is not a linear checklist executed once. It is a rapid, iterative loop. The leader runs the simulation, finds the weak points, refines the approach, and runs it again. By the time they step into the room, they have already navigated the most likely objections and pressure-tested their own assumptions. The result is not rigidity but resilience. They are not performing from a script; they are leading from a position of deep preparation, ready to adapt in real time without ever losing sight of the objective. This is the source of the leader's composure under pressure, and their ability to impose clarity on chaos.

The Call to Action: Auditing Your Own Loop

The journey to becoming an architect of this high-performance system begins not with a grand new initiative, but with a quiet act of self-awareness. For the next week, your task is not to change how you lead, but to simply observe it through the lens of the OODA-EPIQUE framework.

Identify a single, significant leadership challenge you are currently facing and, as you navigate it, consciously audit your own loop. When you gathered information (Observe), did you apply the three lenses of the macro-environment, the competitive arena, and your internal reality, or did you rely on a narrower set of data? As you made sense of it (Orient), did you ground yourself in the brutal facts of Pragmatism and map the human impact with Systemic Empathy? Before committing (Decide), did you pressure-test the choice for bias and consequences (Quality) while building genuine buy-in (Engagement)? Finally, as you moved to execution (Act), did you frame the action as the first turn of a Flywheel, or did the plan's energy dissipate into the daily whirlwind?

This is not an exercise in judgment, but in diagnosis. By seeing where your loop is strong and where it is weak, you identify the precise starting point for your work as an architect.

Pocket Summary

- **Leadership is Adaptation.** The modern leader›s primary role is to navigate complexity. The OODA Loop (Observe, Orient, Decide, Act) is the battle-tested operating system for this task.

- **EPIQUE is the Engine.** The EPIQUE framework is the high-performance engine installed within the OODA loop. It provides the «how» for each «what,» transforming the cycle from a simple process into a powerful cadence of elite performance.

- **Orchestrating the Loop.**

- Observe with Pragmatism. Use rigorous frameworks (PESTLE, Five/Six Forces, VRIO) to build an evidence-based model of reality.

- Orient with Systemic Empathy. Map the human, political, and structural landscape surrounding the facts to gain strategic insight.

- Decide with Quality and Engagement. Pressure-test choices against bias and consequences, while building deep organizational commitment.

- Act with Innovation. Use the clarity and commitment from the OOD stages to ignite a self-reinforcing Flywheel of momentum.

- **The Conductor's Mindset.** The ultimate act of leadership is to internalize this rhythm, conducting both the external actions of the organization and the inner rehearsal of your own thinking to achieve a state of masterful, adaptive execution.

Three Questions for Your Team

1. When we reflect on our last major strategic decision, which phase of our decision-making loop—Observing reality, Orienting ourselves, Deciding on a path, or Acting on it—was the weakest link in our process?

2. Of the five EPIQUE habits, which one is least developed in our team's collective muscle memory, and how does that show up in our daily work?

3. Are we more skilled at executing our current plan with excellence (running today's business) or at adapting and building the plan for tomorrow (creating the future business)?

Conclusion: From Cadence to Mastery

This chapter has provided the blueprint for the organization's master engine: The Meta-Flywheel. By infusing the OODA loop with the five EPIQUE questions, you now have a practical method for creating true adaptive momentum—the ability to not just survive, but to thrive and grow amidst uncertainty.

Where you once saw five disconnected drivers, you now see a single, strategic narrative, that is built into the OODA loop. You have moved from going through the process to intentionally extracting optimum value from it. This clarity transforms your leadership. Your actions are no longer a matter of guesswork or intuition; they become a matter of precision. You have the conductor's score for orchestrating this powerful rhythm.

But having the score is not the same as knowing how well your orchestra is playing. An engine, no matter how well-designed, must be monitored. Are you truly living these principles? Is your organization's culture aligned with this new cadence, or is there friction in the system?

The next chapter is designed to answer these questions. It provides the diagnostic tools to reflect on your practices and measure your team's immersion in the EPIQUE culture. It will help you move from understanding the theory to seeing the reality, identifying precisely where the gaps lie, and illuminating what needs to be looked at next. It is time to move from the blueprint of the engine to the instruments on its dashboard.

CHAPTER 7

THE CONDUCTOR'S SCORE: AN ARCHITECTURAL DIAGNOSTIC

In the previous chapter, we integrated the EPIQUE framework into the OODA loop, creating a complete system for adaptive leadership. We now have the architectural blueprint for a high-performance organization.

A blueprint, however, is not the building. The most common point of failure in any complex endeavour is the gap between the design and the reality of its execution. An organization, no matter how well-designed in theory, is subject to operational drift, cultural friction, and the slow erosion of standards. Without a rigorous method of assessment, a leader is flying blind, unable to distinguish between the intended design and the actual state of the structure.

This chapter, therefore, moves from design to diagnosis. It provides the architect's toolkit for assessing the structural integrity of the organization. It is the equivalent of taking core samples, running stress tests, and using thermal imaging to get a true, evidence-based reading of the building's health. The goal is to render a "Conductor's Score"; a clear, data-driven diagnostic that reveals your organization's unique cultural signature.

This is not a one-time audit. It is a recurring discipline that allows you to track progress, identify emerging weaknesses, and continuously refine your leadership. It is time to move from the blueprint to the inspection.

The Three Lenses of Diagnosis: A Unified Field Theory for Culture

A robust diagnosis cannot rely on a single source of truth. It requires a triangulation of data from distinct but interconnected lenses. This is how we move from a simple opinion to an evidence-based conclusion. The true story of your culture is found not just in the lenses themselves, but in the friction between them.

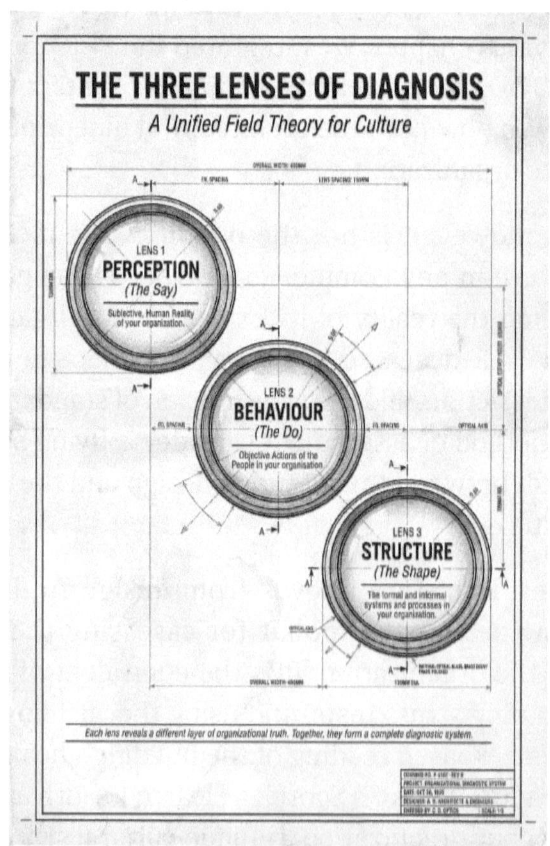

Lens 1: Perception (The "Say"). This is the voice of your people. Through surveys and conversations, it captures how employees perceive the culture. It is the subjective, human reality of your organization.

Lens 2: Behaviour (The "Do"). This lens looks at the objective, verifiable data of what your organization actually does. It analyses project metrics, HR data, meeting minutes, and resource allocation to ground the perceptions in hard evidence.

Lens 3: Structure (The "Shape"). This is the ultimate "why". This lens audits the formal and informal systems, processes, incentives, and symbols that shape and reinforce behaviour. It is the architecture of the anthill.

The Power of the Gaps: Where the Real Story Lives

The most profound insights emerge when we analyse the friction between these lenses. These gaps tell us not just what is happening, but why our efforts to change are failing.

The Credibility Gap: The space between "Say" and "Do". This is the gap between what leaders say is important (Perception) and what the organization actually does (Behaviour). When leaders talk about valuing innovation, but teams see no new exploratory projects being funded, a Credibility Gap opens. This gap is the single fastest destroyer of employee trust and engagement. It breeds cynicism and teaches people to listen to the organization's actions, not its words. A wide Credibility Gap is a sign of a culture that is not living its values.

The Gravity Gap: The space between "Do" and "Shape". This is the gap between the desired behaviours (Do) and the underlying systems (Shape). It explains why change initiatives so often fail and why people go back to old habits even after training. You can exhort your team to be more collaborative (a desired Behaviour), but if your performance review system only rewards individual achievement (a conflicting Structure), the "gravity" of the system will always pull them back to working in silos. A wide Gravity Gap is a sign that your systems are actively working against your strategic goals.

By using this three-lens audit, you move beyond guesswork. You can pinpoint the exact location of your Credibility and Gravity Gaps. You can see not just that your culture is Strained, but that it is strained because your bonus structure is actively undermining your stated value of teamwork. This is the level of diagnostic precision required to make real, lasting change.

Visualizing the Music: The EPIQUE Resonance Profile

The purpose of a good diagnosis isn't to generate a complex report, but to create a single, powerful image that tells a story. We do this using a simple tool for visualizing the music of your culture: the EPIQUE Resonance Profile.

This profile is rendered as a spider chart. Each of the five EPIQUE habits forms an axis, representing a core instrument in your orchestra. Your score is plotted on each axis, and connecting the points reveals your organization's "Cultural Signature".

However, reading this profile requires understanding a crucial principle of conducting: the goal is not to maximize the volume of every instrument; the goal is to achieve a state of dynamic, harmonious balance. An orchestra that is all brass and no strings is simply not an orchestra, just as one that is all strings and no brass.

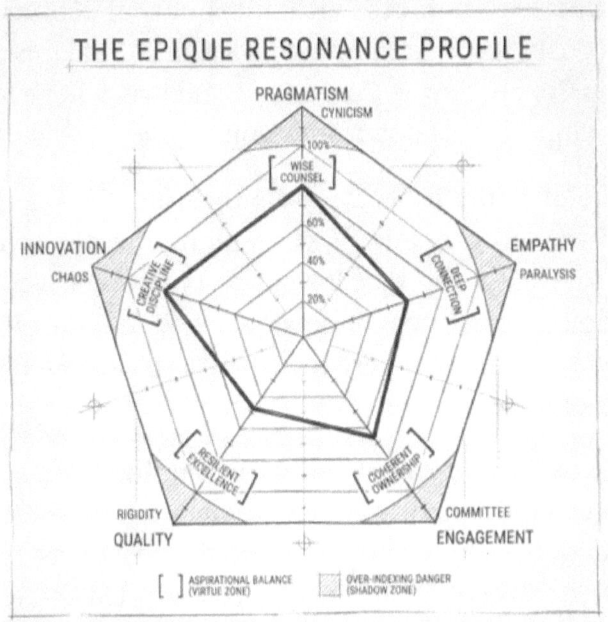

The Path to Virtue: Balancing Strengths to Avoid the Shadows

This leads to the most sophisticated insight the Resonance Profile provides. Every habit, every strength, exists on a spectrum. When a strength is unbalanced by the other habits, it collapses into its negative Shadow. But when it is balanced and integrated with the others, it transcends its basic form and becomes a true Virtue.

The journey to mastery is not just about avoiding the shadows; it is about actively striving for the virtues. The Resonance Profile is your map for this journey.

As the illustration would show, true mastery lies in achieving the balanced state of Virtue. Pushing a strength too far, without the counterbalance of the other habits, causes it to distort into its Shadow. Your goal as a conductor is to guide your organization toward the harmonious expression of these five virtues:

The Virtue of Pragmatism is Wise Counsel. This is the ability to confront brutal facts with Intellectual Honesty while simultaneously inspiring hope and action. It balances realism with vision. Its Shadow is Corrosive Cynicism, where a focus on problems alone grinds down ambition.

The Virtue of Empathy is Deep Connection. This is the ability to understand the needs of your people, stakeholders and customers, while using that insight to make decisive, forward-moving choices. It balances understanding with action. Its Shadow is Consensus-Paralysis, where the desire to please everyone leads to stagnation.

The Virtue of Innovation is Creative Discipline. This is the ability to empower bold Exploration while maintaining the focus and rigor needed to execute and deliver on the best ideas. It balances creativity with execution. Its Shadow is "Shiny Object Syndrome", where a constant search for the new leads to chaos.

The Virtue of Quality is Resilient Excellence. This is the ability to build robust systems that ensure Reliability, while maintaining the flexibility to adapt and improve. It balances process with pragmatism. Its Shadow is Rigid Bureaucracy, where the process becomes more important than the outcome.

The Virtue of Engagement is Coherent Ownership. This is the ability to foster a powerful sense of Shared Purpose while ensuring that clear leadership and decisive action channel that energy effectively. It balances inclusion with direction. Its Shadow is Design by Committee, where too many competing voices lead to a compromised mess.

By framing your goal as the pursuit of these five virtues, your role as a leader becomes clear and aspirational. You are no longer just a manager fixing problems or avoiding risks. You are a conductor, skilfully blending the instruments of your orchestra to transform simple notes into a resonant, harmonious, and truly masterful performance.

The Common Signatures of Dissonance

The interplay between the five habits and their potential for both Virtue and Shadow becomes clear when we examine the common archetypes—the recurring "Cultural Signatures" of dissonance we see time and again. Each archetype tells the story of an organization whose strengths, left unbalanced, have become the very source of its dysfunction.

The "Efficient but Brittle" Fortress. This signature shows high scores in Pragmatism and Quality but low scores in Empathy and Innovation. This organization is excellent at execution, reliable, and disciplined. However, its strengths have failed to achieve their virtuous state. Without the balancing force of Empathy, its Pragmatism has collapsed from the Virtue of *Wise Counsel* into the Shadow of Corrosive Cynicism. Its Quality, without the flexibility of Innovation, has fallen from *Resilient Excellence* into the Shadow of Rigid Bureaucracy. The result is a fortress that is strong today but is actively repelling the very people and ideas it needs to survive tomorrow.

The "Creative but Chaotic" Startup. This signature often shows high scores in Innovation and Engagement but low scores in Quality and Pragmatism. This is a vibrant, exciting place to be, but its strengths are dangerously unbalanced. Its high Innovation has not achieved the Virtue of Creative Discipline; instead, it has fallen into the Shadow of "Shiny Object Syndrome", scattering focus. Its high Engagement, lacking clear direction, has collapsed from Coherent Ownership into the Shadow of Design by Committee. Without the grounding force of Pragmatism and Quality, its brilliant creative energy dissipates before it can be translated into valuable products.

THE TEN SIGNATURES – ARCHETYPES, CONSTRAINTS, AND MULTIPLIER MOVES

1. THE "EFFICIENT BUT BRITTLE" FORTRESS (HIGH PRAGMATISM & QUALITY)

An organization that excels at execution but is slow to adapt. To unlock its potential, you must diagnose its true constraint. If the constraint is Empathy, the multiplier move is to focus on human-centric processes, allowing Quality to mature from Rigid Bureaucracy into Resilient Excellence. If the constraint is Innovation, the move is to provide new, ambitious goals, allowing Pragmatism to mature from Corrosive Cynicism into Wise Counsel. If the constraint is Engagement, the focus must be on building shared purpose, transforming the culture from one of mere compliance into one of pride.

2. THE "BRILLIANT BUT ARROGANT" STRATEGIST (HIGH PRAGMATISM & INNOVATION)

A culture that generates visionary ideas but struggles to connect with people or execute effectively. If the constraint is Empathy, the multiplier move is to ensure brilliant ideas are directed toward solving real customer problems. If the constraint is Engagement, the focus must be on communicating difficult truths in a way that inspires buy-in, not resistance. If the constraint is Quality, the move is to provide the structure needed to mature Innovation from "Shiny Object Syndrome" into the Virtue of Creative Discipline.

3. THE "TRUSTED ADVISOR" (HIGH PRAGMATISM & EMPATHY)

An organization that is wise and understands people but can be slow to act and averse to risk. If the constraint is Innovation, the multiplier move is to provide a new, ambitious path to channel their combined wisdom toward, preventing stagnation. If the constraint is Quality, the focus is on turning good intentions into reliable outcomes, building trust through competence. If the constraint is Engagement, the move is to scale their trusted insights beyond individuals into a sense of Coherent Ownership across the entire organization.

4. THE "PASSIONATE ADVOCATE" (HIGH PRAGMATISM & ENGAGEMENT)

A culture that can rally people around a clear, fact-based mission but may become dogmatic and fail to innovate beyond its current model. If the constraint is Empathy, the multiplier move is to ensure the passionate mission doesn't burn people out, creating a sustainable movement. If the constraint is Innovation, the focus is on opening up new avenues for growth, preventing the organization from becoming a "crusade for a dying cause."
If the constraint is Quality, the move is to channel the passionate energy of Engagement into reliable processes, preventing burnout from heroic efforts.

5. THE "CREATIVE BUT CHAOTIC" STARTUP (HIGH INNOVATION & ENGAGEMENT)

An energetic and passionate organization that lacks focus and struggles with execution. If the constraint is Pragmatism, the multiplier move is to ground creative ideas in market reality, maturing Innovation into Creative Discipline. If the constraint is Quality, the focus is on channeling passionate energy into reliable results, maturing Engagement into Coherent Ownership. If the constraint is Empathy, the move is to direct the organization's creative force toward solving genuine customer problems.

6. THE "IVORY TOWER" ENGINEER (HIGH INNOVATION & QUALITY)

A culture that builds technically sophisticated products but is disconnected from its market and users. If the constraint is Pragmatism, the multiplier move is to prevent "gold-plating" by focusing process rigor only on what the market truly values. If the constraint is Empathy, the focus is on applying technical brilliance to solving real human problems. If the constraint is Engagement, the move is to create a vital feedback loop, allowing market and user insights to flow back into the Innovation and Quality process.

7. THE "EMPATHETIC INVENTOR" (HIGH INNOVATION & EMPATHY)

An organization that deeply understands users and generates creative solutions but struggles to build a viable or scalable business. If the constraint is Pragmatism, the multiplier move is to provide the economic discipline needed to turn a creative idea into a viable business.
If the constraint is Quality, the focus is on delivering the user-centric solution reliably and at scale. If the constraint is Engagement, the move is to rally the organization around the powerful "why" of the customer story, creating Coherent Ownership of the mission.

8. THE "PLEASANT BUT STAGNANT" FAMILY (HIGH EMPATHY & ENGAGEMENT)

A supportive and collaborative culture that avoids conflict and resists change. If the constraint is Pragmatism, the multiplier move is to enable the difficult conversations needed for real change, maturing Empathy from Consensus-Paralysis into Deep Connection. If the constraint is Innovation, the focus is on introducing the "healthy friction" and ambition needed to challenge the comfortable status quo. If the constraint is Quality, the move is to build trust through competence, turning good intentions into reliable outcomes.

9. THE "BURNOUT FACTORY" (HIGH ENGAGEMENT & QUALITY)

A culture of hard-working, committed people who produce excellent work but at an unsustainable pace. If the constraint is Pragmatism, the multiplier move is to ensure process excellence is applied to strategically valuable work, not just busywork. If the constraint is Empathy, the focus is on transforming Engagement from a source of fuel to be burned into a sustainable culture of Coherent Ownership. If the constraint is Innovation, the move is to find smarter, more leveraged ways to achieve results, reducing the reliance on brute-force effort.

10. THE "RESILIENT OPERATOR" (HIGH QUALITY & EMPATHY)

An organization that builds reliable, human-centric systems but may lack a driving, ambitious purpose. If the constraint is Pragmatism, the multiplier move is to ensure that its excellent processes are also economically viable and strategically sound. If the constraint is Innovation, the focus is on providing a new, ambitious goal to which its human-centric systems can be applied. If the constraint is Engagement, the move is to give the well-run, caring system a "why"—a Shared Purpose that elevates the work from a job to a mission.

The "Pleasant but Stagnant" Family. This signature reveals a culture with high scores in Empathy and Engagement but low scores in Pragmatism and Innovation. This is a wonderfully supportive place to work, but its high score in Empathy has not reached the Virtue of Deep Connection. Instead, it has fallen deep into the Shadow of Consensus-Paralysis. To avoid conflict, difficult conversations are avoided, and the organization operates on polite fictions rather than reality. It is a kind and comfortable culture that is slowly suffocating its own future.

The "Burnout Factory". This archetype presents with high Engagement and high Quality but critically low Empathy. Here you have passionate people working incredibly hard to produce excellent work. However, the lack of Empathy means that Engagement never achieves the Virtue of Coherent Ownership. Instead, it becomes a liability—a source of fuel to be consumed. The system runs on the goodwill of its people, treating them as a resource to be burned rather than cultivated, leading inevitably to exhaustion and high turnover.

The "Ivory Tower". This signature shows high Innovation and high Quality but very low Engagement and Empathy. This organization may produce technically brilliant products, but it does so in a vacuum. Its Innovation, lacking the feedback loop of Engagement, fails to achieve the Virtue of Creative Discipline and instead produces solutions for problems that don't exist. Because there is no systemic empathy for the end-user, the products often solve the wrong problems or are difficult to use. It is a culture of brilliant engineering that has lost touch with its market and its own people.

From Signature to Strategy: The Art of the First Move

Seeing your EPIQUE Resonance Profile for the first time is often a glass-shattering moment. It is illuminating, but it can also be overwhelming. The natural instinct is to launch a broad "cultural transformation" that tries to fix everything at once. This is a surefire path to failure; it dilutes resources and creates profound change fatigue.

The true art of leadership is not in doing everything, but in identifying the one move that unlocks all the others.

The Logic of the Bottleneck

To find this leverage point, we turn to a foundational principle of systems thinking, first introduced to the business world in Eliyahu Goldratt's 1984 classic, The Goal: The Theory of Constraints.

While the language may have evolved, Goldratt's core insight—that the output of any complex system is limited by its single greatest bottleneck—remains the intellectual bedrock for many of today's most powerful strategic and operational frameworks. The radical focus demanded by modern goal-setting systems like Objectives and Key Results (OKR) is, in essence, a method for applying resources to a perceived constraint. The rapid, iterative experimentation of the Lean Startup movement, pioneered by Eric Ries, is a high-speed search for the single biggest constraint to growth. Even the core agile practice of identifying and clearing blockers in a sprint is a micro-application of Goldratt's fundamental logic.

These modern methods are powerful, but they are the branches of a tree whose trunk is the Theory of Constraints. By returning to this foundational idea, we gain a clear and timeless diagnostic lens. To create meaningful change, you must first identify and address the system's primary bottleneck. This logic gives you a radical and liberating permission. The permission to temporarily stop polishing your strengths and focus all your energy where it truly matters.

The Multiplier Effect: Unlocking the Path to Virtue

This feels counter-intuitive. Why would you ignore what you're good at? The answer is that an unbalanced strength cannot achieve its virtuous state. It remains trapped as a dysfunctional shadow. Pouring more energy into a strength that is already in its shadow doesn't just fail to help; it can be actively destructive. For an organization already suffering from "Shiny Object Syndrome," more innovation workshops only deepen the chaos.

Your first move is therefore to focus on the Constraining Habit. This is the Multiplier Move. It doesn't diminish your strengths; it creates the balance needed for them to finally mature from their Shadow into their true Virtue.

Mapping Your Leverage Point

An archetype is a pattern of symptoms defined by its high- and low-scoring habits. If an organization is strong in two habits, its primary bottleneck—its Constraining Habit—will logically be one of the other three. Your three-lens diagnostic is what allows you to pinpoint which of these is the true bottleneck holding back the entire system.

The table illustrates this. It shows how the archetypes, when defined clearly by their constraining habits, allows you to make a Multiplier Move that unlocks the path to Virtue for your existing strengths.

Conclusion: The System's First Move

This chapter has moved the focus from architectural design to diagnostic inspection. The result is a complete system for assessing an organization's true cultural signature: a three-lens audit to gather the data, the EPIQUE Resonance Profile to visualize the patterns, and the Theory of Constraints to find the point of maximum leverage.

This provides a profound shift in organizational self-awareness. The organization is no longer just reacting to symptoms or launching broad, unfocused initiatives. It now possesses a precise diagnostic capability, allowing it to see the hidden structural forces that shape its performance. It can understand not just that it is struggling, but that its high Engagement is being undermined by a lack of Pragmatic focus, creating the "Burnout Factory" archetype. The strategic path forward becomes clear: the solution is not another engagement survey, but a targeted intervention to strengthen the constraining habit of Pragmatism.

This is the essence of a strategically mature organization. It is the ability to analyse a complex system, identify the primary source of dissonance, and know with clarity and confidence which single capability requires development. This grants the organization the strategic patience to stop over-investing in its dominant strengths and the focused courage to address its primary bottleneck. This first, deliberate move is what begins the process of rebalancing the system, allowing its shadow strengths to finally mature into their virtuous forms.

But diagnosis, no matter how precise, is not action. The final step is to translate this systemic insight into a concrete plan. The next and final chapter will provide the guide for this work, laying out how to use these diagnostic findings to architect a targeted, high-leverage intervention—the organization's first move in the continuous and rewarding work of building a masterpiece.

CHAPTER 8

THE FIRST PUSH: A PLAYBOOK FOR YOUR ARCHETYPE

We have travelled a great distance together. We began with the five core habits of the EPIQUE framework. We then placed them in the dynamic rhythm of the OODA Loop, building the master engine of adaptation: the **Meta-Flywheel**. In the last chapter, we created the diagnostic tools to render your unique **Cultural Signature**, using the Theory of Constraints to identify your organization's single point of maximum leverage—its primary Constraining Habit.

You have moved from philosophy to process, and from process to diagnosis. You may now know, with evidence-based clarity, that your organization is a "Brilliant but Arrogant Strategist" constrained by a lack of Engagement, or a "Pleasant but Stagnant Family" held back by a deficit of Pragmatism.

This is the moment where all that intellectual work culminates in a single, critical question: "What do I do now?"

This chapter provides the answer. It is the bridge from insight to impact. It provides a specific, tailored playbook for making the first push on your Meta-Flywheel by addressing the one habit that is holding your entire system back.

This is not a generic guide to change management. It is a set of precise interventions designed for your specific diagnosis. For any given constraint, the work is always the same: you must pull three levers of change in a coordinated and relentless campaign. These levers are:

1. **The Leader's Stance.** You must personally model the new behaviour, using clear signals and relentless consistency to prove the change is real and recalibrate the organization's risk-reward calculus.

2. **The Architecture of Habit.** You must become a systems architect, reshaping the environment by adding friction to the old ways of working and removing it from the new.

3. **The Evidence Locker.** You must act as a curator, building an unassailable case for the new way of working by amplifying verifiable narratives and empowering local champions.

The following sections are organized by your diagnosed Constraining Habit. Turn to the playbook that matches your Cultural Signature. This is your first move. This is how you begin.

The Playbook for a PRAGMATISM Constraint

If your diagnosis has revealed that your organization's Constraining Habit is **Pragmatism**, you are likely leading a "Creative but Chaotic" Startup or a "Pleasant but Stagnant" Family. Your culture excels at generating ideas or maintaining harmony, but it avoids difficult truths and is unmoored from reality. Your "First Push" on the Meta-Flywheel must be a relentless campaign to instil intellectual honesty. This requires a coordinated intervention across the three levers of change.

Your campaign begins with **The Leader's Stance**. You must personally and publicly model the very behaviour you wish to see, recalibrating the organization's risk-reward calculus. The most powerful move is to find an opportunity to publicly admit a significant personal mistake or a deeply held wrong assumption. This act serves as a costly signal, proving you are willing to sacrifice your own status in service of the truth. You must follow this by killing a popular "pet project"—perhaps even your own—that the data clearly shows is failing. This demonstrates that facts, not feelings or politics, now govern decisions. In every meeting, you must relentlessly ask, "What is the data telling us?" and "What is the brutal truth we are all avoiding right now?", refusing to proceed until you get a fact-based answer. This consistent behaviour makes it clear that the price of avoiding reality has become uncomfortably high.

Next, you must re-architect the environment to make pragmatism the path of least resistance. This is the work on the **Architecture of Habit**. You must attack the systems that allow polite fictions to survive. The most effective intervention is to implement blameless post-mortems or after-action reviews for all significant projects, successful or not. This creates a formal, safe system for dissecting the truth of what really happened. You must also change the sanctions. Make it an explicit policy, reinforced in performance reviews, that failing to raise a known risk is a far more serious offense than having a project fail for well-documented reasons. This fundamentally alters the incentive structure, making silence more dangerous than dissent. Symbolically, you can create an award for the "Truth-Teller of the Quarter," celebrating those who bring forward uncomfortable but vital information, signalling that this behaviour is now the new standard of excellence.

Finally, you must build the **Evidence Locker** to make the shift irreversible. You cannot simply declare a new era of pragmatism; you must prove it with verifiable narratives. Find a team that, using the new blameless post-mortem system, made a difficult but honest pivot away from a failing strategy. Your role is not to tell their story for them, but to empower the team lead as a local champion. Give them the stage at the next town hall to present their journey, focusing not on the failure but on the intelligence of their decision to change course. This narrative, backed by the proof of your own stance and the new post-mortem system, becomes an unassailable piece of evidence. It demonstrates to the entire organization that pragmatism is not just a new slogan, but the new, rewarded, and rational way of working.

The Playbook for an EMPATHY Constraint

If your diagnosis has revealed that your organization's primary constraint is **Empathy**, you are likely at the helm of an "Efficient but Brittle" Fortress, a "Burnout Factory," or a "Brilliant but Arrogant" Strategist. Your culture may be excellent at execution or strategy, but it is disconnected from its people and its customers, leading to rigidity and exhaustion. Your "First Push" on the Meta-Flywheel must be a deliberate campaign to infuse the system with a deep, operational understanding of human needs.

As before, this campaign begins with **The Leader's Stance**. The principles of recalibrating risk through costly signals and consistency remain the same, but the application is different. Your most powerful costly signal is the sacrifice of your own time and status. Clear your calendar for an entire day to do nothing but listen, without a fixed agenda, to your most frustrated customers or your most stressed frontline employees. This act demonstrates that their perspective is now more valuable than your executive schedule. Follow this by publicly changing a major decision—one that was analytically sound—based on new information about its negative human impact. This proves that "people impact" is no longer a soft variable but a hard input in your decision-making calculus. Your consistent behaviour must be to ask in every strategy review, "How does this affect our customers?" and "What is the experience of the team that has to build this?", making these questions a non-negotiable part of the process.

With your stance established, you must reshape the **Architecture of Habit** to make empathy systemic, not just personal. The goal is to hardwire the "voice of the other" into the organization's daily rhythm. The most potent symbolic act is to begin every single senior leadership meeting with a five-minute "Voice of the Customer" story—a recording, a letter, a direct quote—making it the most sacred ritual of the week. You must then attack the systems. Integrate customer satisfaction scores or employee well-being metrics directly into the performance scorecards for every leader in the organization, making empathy a key indicator of success. To remove friction for this new behaviour, create a direct, unfiltered channel—like a dedicated Slack channel or a monthly "customer council"—where engineers and strategists can hear directly from users without the information being sanitized by layers of management.

Finally, you build the **Evidence Locker** to amplify the change. Your aim is to find a verifiable narrative that proves listening leads to winning. Identify a recent product change or a process improvement that was directly inspired by feedback from your new listening systems. Your role is not to claim credit, but to find the local champion—the customer service manager whose team first raised the issue, or the product manager who fought for the change. Empower them to present the story at the next all-hands meeting. This narrative, backed by the proof of your own listening tour and the new "Voice of the Customer" ritual, becomes an unassailable testament. It proves to the entire organization that empathy is not about being "nice"; it is a rigorous, rewarded discipline that creates better products and a healthier culture.

The Playbook for an ENGAGEMENT Constraint

If your diagnosis points to Engagement as your primary constraint, you are likely leading a "Brilliant but Arrogant" Strategist or an "Ivory Tower" Engineer. Your organization operates in a top-down manner, failing to harness the collective intelligence of its people. Your "First Push" on the Meta-Flywheel must be a campaign to prove that good ideas are valued regardless of where they come from.

This campaign begins with **The Leader's Stance**. Instead of waiting for a good idea to emerge, you proactively create one. Your costly signal is a deliberate investment of your own time and authority in junior talent. Form a small, cross-functional "tiger team" of high-potential staff to tackle a real strategic problem, and personally mentor them. The crucial act is to then publicly champion and allocate a pilot budget for their best idea, proving you are not just looking for good ideas, but are actively cultivating them from every level.

Next, you re-engineer **The Architecture of Habit** to create systemic pathways for upward communication. A powerful symbolic change is to dedicate time in every town hall to a live, unvetted "Ask Me Anything" session, proving no topic is off-limits. The most crucial systemic intervention is to institute "skip-level" meetings, where you meet directly with frontline staff purely to listen. This creates a formal, low-friction channel for unfiltered truth to travel upwards, and you must visibly reward the leaders whose teams are most praised for their candour in these sessions.

Finally, you build **The Evidence Locker** by making the "tiger team's" success a legendary and verifiable narrative. Your role is to move from being the team's private mentor to their public sponsor. Give them the main stage at the next company-wide meeting to present their journey and the impact of the pilot program you funded. This story, backed by the proof of your investment (The Stance) and the new open channels (The Architecture), becomes an unassailable signal. It proves to everyone that speaking up is not a career risk, but a genuine opportunity to shape the future of the company.

The Playbook for an INNOVATION Constraint

If your diagnosis reveals Innovation as your primary constraint, you are likely leading an "Efficient but Brittle" Fortress or a "Pleasant but Stagnant" Family. Your culture is excellent at optimizing the present but is risk-averse and fails to create the future. Your "First Push" on the Meta-Flywheel must be a campaign to make exploration safe and productive.

Your intervention begins with **The Leader's Stance**. Your costly signal must be a public embrace of intelligent risk. Find a small, strategically aligned but unproven project and publicly fund it. Crucially, you must state that you are funding the learning, not the immediate ROI, and that the "cost" of the experiment is a worthy price for the knowledge it will generate. This act demonstrates that you are willing to sacrifice short-term predictability for long-term discovery. Your consistency test is to then protect this team from premature scrutiny, celebrating their learning milestones, even if their initial hypotheses fail.

Next, you reshape **The Architecture of Habit** to create protected spaces for new ideas. The most powerful systemic intervention is to carve out a small, "no-questions-asked" experimental fund that teams can access without going through the standard, rigorous budget approval process. This creates a low-friction path for early-stage exploration. To change the sanctions, you must attack the stigma of failure. A potent symbolic act is to create a "Glorious Failure of the Month" award, given not for mistakes, but for the team that ran the most elegant experiment that produced the most valuable (and often surprising) learning. This reframes failure from a career risk to a mark of honour.

Finally, you build **The Evidence Locker** with a verifiable narrative of productive failure. The story you must amplify is that of the team who received the first "Glorious Failure" award. Your role is to sponsor this narrative, giving the team lead a platform to explain their hypothesis, how they tested it, what they learned when it broke, and how that learning is now saving the company from making a much larger, more expensive mistake. This story, backed by the proof of your own investment in risky projects and the new experimental fund, becomes an unassailable testament. It proves to the entire organization that the path to success is paved with intelligent, well-executed experiments.

The Playbook for an ENGAGEMENT Constraint

If your diagnosis points to **Engagement** as your primary constraint, you are likely leading a "Brilliant but Arrogant" Strategist or an "Ivory Tower" Engineer. Your organization may be strategically or technically excellent, but it operates in a top-down manner, failing to harness the collective intelligence of its people. Your "First Push" on the Meta-Flywheel must be a campaign to prove that good ideas are valued regardless of where they come from.

Your intervention starts with **The Leader's Stance**. Your costly signal must be a deliberate and visible investment of your own time and authority in junior talent. Instead of waiting for a good idea to emerge, you must proactively create it. Form a small, cross-functional "tiger team" of high-potential junior staff, tasked with tackling a real, meaningful strategic problem. Personally mentor this team, giving them direct access to your thinking and creating a safe space for them to develop their ideas.

The crucial moment comes when this team presents its findings. Your role is to listen intently and then, in a public forum, champion their best idea, even if it challenges the status quo or a more senior leader's position. You must allocate a real, albeit small, budget to pilot their proposal, stating clearly, "This team has done the work, their logic is sound, and we are backing them." This act of sponsorship—investing your time in mentorship and your political capital in their idea—is a far more powerful signal than a thousand speeches on empowerment. It proves you are not just looking for good ideas, but are actively cultivating them from every level of the organization.

Next, you re-engineer the **Architecture of Habit** to create systemic pathways for upward communication. The goal is to dismantle the invisible walls that keep leadership insulated. A powerful symbolic change is to dedicate the first 15 minutes of every town hall to a live, unvetted "Ask Me Anything" session, proving that no topic is off-limits. The most crucial systemic intervention is to institute "skip-level" meetings, where you meet directly with the reports of your direct reports, not to micromanage, but purely to listen. This creates a formal, low-friction channel for unfiltered truth to travel upwards. To change the sanctions, you must visibly reward and promote leaders who are praised by their own teams for their willingness to listen and elevate their people's ideas.

Finally, you build the **Evidence Locker** with a verifiable narrative of bottom-up impact. Find a clear example where a suggestion from a skip-level meeting or an "Ask Me Anything" session directly led to a significant, positive change in company policy, product strategy, or employee benefits. Your role is to sponsor this story. Identify the employee who made the original suggestion and empower them as your local champion. Work with them to write a post for the company intranet or have them briefly share their experience at the next all-hands meeting. This story, backed by the proof of your own public deference to better ideas and the new skip-level meeting system, becomes an unassailable signal. It proves to everyone that speaking up is not a career risk, but a genuine opportunity to shape the future of the company.

The Playbook for a QUALITY Constraint

If your diagnosis points to **Quality** as your primary constraint, you are likely leading a "Creative but Chaotic" Startup or a "Passionate Advocate" organization. Your culture is full of energy and good intentions, but it lacks the discipline to deliver reliable, excellent outcomes. Your "First Push" on the Meta-Flywheel must be a campaign to make discipline a non-negotiable value.

This campaign begins with **The Leader's Stance**. Your costly signal must be a public sacrifice of speed in the name of excellence. The most powerful move is to personally halt a major, highly anticipated product launch or initiative because you have identified a potential quality flaw. You must publicly take the heat for the delay, stating clearly that "shipping on time with a flaw is not an option". This act proves that you value the integrity of the work over the pressure of the deadline. Your consistency test is to then relentlessly praise and promote the meticulous, detail-oriented "finishers" over the fast-moving "starters."

Next, you must re-engineer the **Architecture of Habit** to build discipline directly into the workflow. The most crucial systemic intervention is to grant frontline teams the authority—and the obligation—to "pull the Andon cord" and stop a process the moment they spot a defect, without fear of reprisal. This distributes ownership of quality to the people closest to the work. To change the sanctions, you must make quality a primary criterion for advancement. Visibly promote a respected engineer known for their meticulous, reliable work over a "fast-shipper" who leaves a trail of technical debt. This symbolic act sends a clear message about what is truly valued.

Finally, you build the **Evidence Locker** with a verifiable narrative of how discipline prevented disaster. Find a clear example where a team used their new "stop the line" authority to halt a process, identify a critical flaw, and ultimately save the company from a major customer-facing failure or a costly recall. Your role is to sponsor this story. Empower the team lead or a respected senior engineer to explain what happened, not as a story of delay, but as a story of professional excellence and proactive problem-solving. This narrative, backed by the proof of your own willingness to delay a launch and the new authority you have granted to teams, becomes an unassailable testament. It proves that quality is not a bureaucratic burden, but the ultimate expression of respect for the customer and for the craft itself.

Conclusion: From a Single Push to Unstoppable Momentum

This three-part intervention—recalibrating risk through your **Stance**, redesigning the **Architecture of Habit**, and building an **Evidence Locker** of verifiable narratives—is the complete engine of the "First Push." It is a repeatable, disciplined process for turning a single diagnostic insight into a tangible cultural shift.

But its true power lies beyond the immediate improvement of your Constraining Habit. A successful first push does more than just improve one score on your Cultural Signature. It achieves something far more valuable: it breaks the organizational cynicism that so often suffocates change. It proves to your people, through irrefutable evidence, that change is not just another slogan, but a new market reality within the firm. It builds not just belief, but a new set of rational expectations.

This initial victory, however small, infuses the entire system with a new sense of agency. It creates the initial momentum that makes the second push on the Meta-Flywheel—targeting the next constraint—easier, faster, and more powerful. You have now completed the full cycle of the EPIQUE operating system: you have diagnosed your reality, identified your leverage point, and executed a successful, evidence-based intervention. You have the complete blueprint for transformation.

FINDING YOUR FOOTING IN THE STORM

This journey began with a simple, honest admission: leading today often feels like trying to conduct an orchestra in the middle of a storm. The noise of daily urgencies is overwhelming, the old music of predictable strategy no longer works, and the baton of leadership can feel broken in your hand. We started by asking a fundamental question: In a world defined by permanent chaos, how do we find a way to lead effectively again, not just to survive, but to create and thrive?

This book was architected to provide a clear and practical answer to that question.

The first part of our journey, therefore, was about forging a new and more relevant set of tools. But before we could build anything, we had to stop talking about "disruption" as a vague, catch-all term and instead accurately diagnose the storm we are all navigating. We came to understand that it is not a single event, but a persistent, five-front storm that now defines the modern business world. Naming these fronts is the first step toward conquering them.

First, we face **The End of the Five-Year Plan**. This is the humbling reality that our traditional methods of long-range strategic planning are broken. We can no longer confidently plot a course, years into the future. As the landscape shifts under our feet with dizzying speed, this approach can be misleading. Our carefully crafted plans, once a source of stability, now feel like a source of fragility, shattering against the relentless waves of unpredictable technological, social, and economic change. Second, we are confronted by **Losing Touch with Customers**. Their needs, desires, and behaviours now evolve faster than our annual surveys and focus groups can track. The assumptions that built our most successful products have grown stale, leaving us at risk of building perfectly engineered solutions for problems that no longer exist. This is coupled with the third front: **Outdated Ways of Working**. The rigid, siloed, and slow-moving processes that were designed for efficiency in a predictable world now actively prevent us from adapting. They have become the bars of a cage, trapping our talent and preventing the speed and creativity needed to keep pace.

Internally, these external pressures have given rise to two more fronts. We must mend **The Motivation Crisis**. In a world of constant change and uncertainty, the old contract of a steady pay check for compliant work is no longer enough. People feel disconnected from the mission, cynical about leadership, and uninspired by their daily tasks, leading to a quiet epidemic of disengagement. Underlying all of this is the fifth and most corrosive front: **The Trust Deficit**. Decades of reorganizations, broken promises, and a focus on short-term results have eroded the trust between leaders and employees, between departments, and even between colleagues. This lack of trust is a tax on every single transaction. It makes collaboration political, discourages honest feedback, and makes the kind of intelligent risk-taking required for innovation nearly impossible.

Having named the true nature of the storm, the path forward is not to find five separate solutions for five separate problems. A fragmented approach cannot solve a systemic crisis. Instead, the work is to cultivate a new set of core organizational capabilities—a single, integrated framework of mutually reinforcing habits. This is the core logic of the EPIQUE framework. It is not a list of antidotes; it is a recipe for building a fundamentally stronger and more adaptive organization. The goal is not to patch the holes in the ship, but to re-architect the vessel so it is designed for the storm from the keel up.

When these habits are woven into the fabric of an organization, they create a new, emergent state of being. The relentless discipline of **Pragmatism** instils an institutional honesty, grounding every conversation and decision in the bedrock of reality. This creates a culture that is allergic to wishful thinking and polite fictions, giving it the stability to navigate uncertainty without losing its footing. Upon this foundation, **Systemic Empathy** acts as the organization's sensory system, allowing it to feel the subtle shifts in the market and the deep, unmet needs of its customers. It also allows the organization to feel the friction within its own walls, seeing its people not as resources to be managed, but as the very heart of its adaptive capacity.

This awareness is then channelled by the habit of **Engagement**, which is the architectural work of creating shared purpose and coherent ownership. It transforms a collection of individuals into a committed crew, focused on a common destination. This collective energy is then given a direction for discovery by the habit of **Innovation**, which provides the disciplined engine for exploring new possibilities, testing assumptions, and creating novel solutions. Finally, the entire system is bound together by the character of **Quality**—a deep, pervasive commitment to excellence, responsibility, and trust. It is the integrity of the system that ensures its actions are not just clever, but also wise, and that its promises are always kept.

The EPIQUE habits, therefore, are not five separate tools. They are a tightly woven system of thought and action. By cultivating them in concert, an organization doesn't just solve its current problems; it fundamentally upgrades its operating system. It builds the enduring, adaptive capacity to handle the next storm, and the one after that, not by reacting, but by being a different kind of organization altogether.

But possessing this new toolkit is not enough if the organization lacks a coherent way to wield it, or a clear place to begin. This was the purpose of the second part of the book. It was designed to provide a new mindset and a practice-based start point. We saw how the EPIQUE habits could be woven into the simple, powerful rhythm of the **OODA Loop**, giving the organization a new cadence for thinking and acting its way through complexity.

This moved the habits from a static list into a dynamic, integrated system for execution. More importantly, the **Conductor's Score** provided a rigorous diagnostic tool; a way to look at the organization through a clear lens and, for the first time, see a coherent picture of its unique strengths and dysfunctions. It answered the most pressing and paralyzing question of all, "With so much to fix, where do we possibly start?". By identifying the primary bottleneck, the "Constraining Habit", it revealed the one place where a small, focused effort could create the biggest possible impact. This answers the how and where to begin.

Now, we must address the most pragmatic challenge of all, the one that every leader faces after closing a book like this. Knowing what to do and how to begin is not the same as doing it. The inertia of an organization is a powerful force. The daily whirlwind of meetings, emails, and urgent tasks will try to pull everyone back into old, familiar habits. Your people, having seen countless change initiatives come and go, are likely armed with a healthy dose of scepticism. A book, no matter how insightful, cannot magically change a culture.

A cultural pivot is not a single event; it is a continuous, often quiet, act of persistence. It is not a revolution launched with a grand announcement and a new set of posters for the wall. It is an evolution that begins by changing the conversation. It is the choice, in one budget meeting, to ask a more pragmatic question about the evidence behind an assumption. It is the decision, in one coaching session, to patiently guide a team member with more empathy instead of just giving them the answer. It is the courage, in one project review, to celebrate the valuable learning from a failure instead of just judging the missed deadline.

This is where the real work lies, and it is work that is both smaller and harder than we might imagine. It is less about being a heroic conductor launching a grand symphony, and more about being a patient gardener, tending to the soil day after day, week after week. You start by improving the health of one small patch—the area identified by your diagnostic as your greatest constraint. You focus your energy there, proving to a small group that a new way of working can yield better results and, just as importantly, feel more meaningful for the people doing it. Success in one area creates curiosity in others. A small, undeniable win builds the credibility needed for a slightly bigger one. This is how real, lasting change takes root.

The blueprint is now yours. We began by acknowledging that we are no longer in a merely VUCA world, but a BANI one—a world that is Brittle, Anxious, Non-linear, and Incomprehensible. The EPIQUE framework was architected for this reality. It is a system designed not to predict the unpredictable, but to build organizations with the inherent resilience to thrive when systems are **Brittle**. It fosters the psychological safety and shared purpose that calms a culture of **Anxiety**. It provides the adaptive cadence of the OODA loop to navigate a **Non-linear** world where cause and effect are disconnected. And it offers the diagnostic clarity of the Conductor's Score to bring a measure of sense-making to an otherwise **Incomprehensible** environment.

The storm will not end, but you no longer need to feel lost within it. You have a way to find your footing, a way to read the new weather, and a clear, logical place to begin the work. The journey ahead is not easy, but it is no longer a mystery.

Start there.

AUTHOR'S BACKGROUND

Jeevaganth is a values-driven senior leader who has spent over three decades navigating the intersections of complexity, transformation, and community stewardship. His career is defined by guiding diverse organizations through pivotal change—from architecting a new office within the Singapore Public Service to leading a statutory body through transformation.

His expertise is grounded in both strategic theory and on-the-ground execution. With a background that spans military, private-sector, and public service leadership, he has consistently been tasked with translating high-level intent into operational reality.

A dedicated synthesizer, and systems thinker, he has pursued knowledge in contrasting domains — from engineering and defence technology to business administration and career counselling — always seeking to connect rigorous frameworks with the pragmatic, people-centric work of building resilient and innately adaptive organizations.

www.ingramcontent.com/pod-product-compliance
Lightning Source LLC
Chambersburg PA
CBHW022057050726
47591CB00002B/578